"I'm so glad I read *The Achiever Fever Cure*. Aside from being hilarious and entertaining, it has helped me better understand what really drives me and I have become much more aware of the stories I tell myself. Thank you, Claire, for being so honest and open, and for sharing your enlightening journey with us!"

—**CHARLES CHANG**, founder of plant-protein brand Vega; founder and President, Lyra Growth Partners

"Booth's raw journey spoke to me in an approachable way. She shares the tools and systems she discovered to ease the intensity of 'achiever fever' and manages to do it while building and growing her business with soulful intention."

—**JODY SHAKESPEARE**, BJL Coaching and Consulting

"*The Achiever Fever Cure* provides a hands-on framework for those of us who want to strive less and thrive more."

—**LISA MARTIN**, founder of FLOURISH for Female Leaders and author of *Briefcase Moms*

"It didn't take me too many pages to realize that I was no longer reading about Claire Booth's struggle but about myself. This is a courageous book, born of sincerity and caring. It is a cathartic read... I realize now that I am not alone."

—**TERENCE WALLIS**, author of *Indelible Adventures*

"We follow Booth through a life journey that is all too common—a journey of striving, struggle, and burnout. We laugh and cry with her as she tells her story with warmth and determination. A truly wonderful and insightful book."

—**YURI FULMER**, Chairman, Fulmer Capital Partners

THE
ACHIEVER
FEVER
CURE

How I Learned To Stop
Striving Myself Crazy

CLAIRE BOOTH

Published by LifeTree Media Ltd.
lifetreemedia.com

Distributed by Greystone Books Ltd.
greystonebooks.com

Cataloguing data available from Library and Archives Canada.

ISBN: 978-1-928055-35-8 (paperback)
ISBN: 978-1-928055-36-5 (EPUB)
ISBN: 978-1-928055-37-2 (PDF)

Grateful acknowledgement is made to the following sources. In the event of an inadvertent omission or error, please notify the publisher.

Permission to reprint material from www.thework.com graciously provided by Byron Katie and Stephen Mitchell. Readers are invited to visit the website for more information about The Work.

Permission to reprint material from *The One You Feed* podcast graciously provided by Eric Zimmer, theoneyoufeed.net.

Cover and interior design by Greg Tabor
Cover illustration © Aeriform

Printed and bound in Canada.

To Kate and Esther

TABLE OF CONTENTS

INTRODUCTION

THE NIGHTS ARE the worst.

As I set my alarm, I do the math on how many hours of sleep I can get: ten o'clock now, asleep by ten thirty, up at 5:30 am, that's seven hours, plenty of time. I check my email one last time, turn the light off, and remind myself that tonight does not have to go like last night, or the night before that. Given how sleep-deprived I am, I feel like I'm ahead of the game—I'm bound to sleep well. I've got this, I tell myself.

As I settle down under the covers, I think back through the day, checking that everything got done: Did that... yep... got that. Missed that thing... gotta get that on the agenda for tomorrow... oh but I have that other thing... and what about.... And then I catch myself. Enough! Stop! Go to sleep!

I roll over and try to think about nothing but soon thoughts are rolling in like a thick fog—thoughts about hiring, closing sales, and reaching quarterly revenue targets. My thoughts blend together in a soupy worry that I slosh around in for an hour or so until the "big gun" thoughts rise from the depths:

What's wrong with you? You need to try harder. You need to be better. They're going to think you don't know what you're doing.

It's midnight now and my breathing is shallow, my chest feels hollow, and my stomach has clenched up. I command myself to stop the thinking, stop the worrying, but I'm under a spell. I have no ability to break through this incessant thought stream that will keep me up tonight, just like it did the previous night. I spend the next few hours tossing and turning until I'm an angry, despairing, sweaty, feverish mess. Then I throw other concerns into the pot—the crappy workout I'm going to have the next morning, the idea that my financial advisor might be ripping me off, the fact that I haven't called my parents in three weeks. Eventually, I'll fall asleep and have the dream where I'm in high school and realize the night before the exam that I forgot to attend science that semester.

This doesn't happen every night, but I used to go through waves of nights like this several times a year and they tended to happen whenever business was down. I own a market research agency and our revenues are dependent on client work. We need to delight our current clients so they keep coming back, as well as ensure the pipeline of potential business stays full. Every so often, like in any small business, the emails slow to a dribble and the phone goes quiet. After almost twenty years of experience in my industry, I understand intellectually and rationally that there are ebbs and flows and that the work will eventually pick up. But my reaction was always the same: I cast myself as the villain responsible for the slowdown. I would remind my team that this was a short-term lull and to take advantage of the downtime, but instead of taking my own advice, all I heard in my head was: You are failing! You don't know what you're doing! You've got to try harder! I imagined letting all my employees go, filing for bankruptcy, and ending up a haggard old woman sleeping under a bridge.

Nothing in my life explained my extreme reactions. I wasn't ill or had committed any crimes. The business I had started five years previously was flourishing and growing at an average of twenty-five percent each year. At work, I was surrounded by a team of bright, caring co-workers who treated each other like family. At home, I lived with my partner of fifteen years, Chris, an executive at a technology firm who loved nothing more than to be outside fly fishing and skiing. I was close to my parents and my two younger sisters were my best friends. I had three hilarious nephews and was a Big Sister to a smart, fun-loving teenage girl. Physically, I was in good health and took my fitness seriously. Most mornings before work, I'd either be in the pool with my Masters swim team or climbing at the local climbing gym. Since I had no kids, I had plenty of downtime to read, travel, hang out with girlfriends, and binge watch the occasional TV show.

But I lived in a state of urgency, trying to constantly improve. I'm an achiever and have been an achiever all my life. I'm driven, ambitious, competitive, and I like to lead. I have very high expectations of myself and am proud of my achievements: my education, my career, the company I've built. Being an achiever has given me some very useful character traits like discipline, a desire to excel, a strong work ethic, and persistence, but it has also infected me with an unrelenting need to strive, improve, and grow.

Achievers are happiest when they are achieving. This phenomenon bore out when I surveyed two hundred self-identified achievers during the writing of this book, and ninety percent of them agreed that achieving their goals is what makes them happiest. When I turned forty, I should have been happy given that I had achieved most of the goals I had set for myself, but instead, misery was a frequent companion. Once I achieved a goal, I created another. A friend of mine describes this constant goal-seeking as a treadmill that achievers are forever trying to outrun. As we succeed, the incline increases, the speed gets faster, and we either keep running or fall off.

And it gets worse. Achievers also tend to be their own merciless critic. If I wasn't moving ahead, I was going backwards. If I wasn't growing, I was dying. I had to keep achieving because the alternative was unthinkable. This is the dark side of achievement, a sickness I call achiever fever.

Perhaps you have experienced some of its symptoms:
- A strong need to prove yourself
- Measuring worth by accomplishments
- Needing to feel like you have everything under control
- Persistent self-criticism
- Needing to feel productive and terrified of wasting time
- Future-focused
- Fearing you won't live up to your potential
- Habitual worry
- Frequent comparison with others
- Using food and/or alcohol to make yourself feel better

Fevers can bring strange, hallucinatory dreams. And, as I would later come to understand, achiever fever is a powerful delusion. It grips you tightly until you take it upon yourself to break through it. And the only way to break through is to become aware that you are feverish.

The first clue that my own achiever fever was negatively permeating my life was something an employee wrote in my annual leadership review: "I know what kind of a day it's going to be as soon as Claire walks into the office." That sentence was a gut punch. That employee had no idea what I'd done outside the office door—pasting a smile on my face, telling myself to let go of the fatigue induced by insomnia, urging myself to slow down and say a proper "hello" rather than heading straight to my desk and trying to jump start the day. But she saw through the mask. My behaviour was having an impact on her morale and infecting her with my negative energy. This was bad for business.

The second clue was an awareness of a phrase that had taken up residence in my head that same year of my life: I've got to get out of my own way. I wasn't sure what it meant, or where it had come from, but it had been rolling ominously through my thoughts for months, especially when I was angry with myself. All I could hear was that if I could just push through, I'd feel better and success would come more easily.

Several years ago, I was reading Alain de Botton's book, *The Art of Travel*, and the following idea jumped out at me. Hungry for a break from his daily life, de Botton arrives in Barbados only to realize that, along with his luggage, he has also inadvertently packed himself.[1] I saw a parallel between his frustration at being unable to leave himself behind and my inability to get out of my own way. Later I understood how my awareness of this had sparked the process of change, but at the time what was important was that I registered that the cause of my unhappiness was me.

The acknowledgement that I was the cause of my misery, combined with the recognition that my employees could see

5

through my falsely constructed enthusiasm finally caused me to say, enough. I was in danger of becoming a liability to my business. My employees deserved a strong, powerful, confident leader and, if I wanted to keep growing the business, I had to change. I had no idea how, however. I'd never spent any time trying to understand myself.

That's an ironic place to be because, as a market researcher, I'm in the business of understanding people. My job is to look for insights and it's a heady feeling discovering them. I'll be moderating a focus group and a participant will use a word or a phrase that doesn't quite line up with the discussion. At first I feel a physical tingle and I know I'm onto something. Like an archeologist, I carefully examine the participants' words, sweeping off the subconscious layers with well-chosen questions, until, there it is: the "a-ha," a gold nugget, an insight.

A good market researcher is highly intuitive. They know how to be patient, how to listen to what is being said, as well as what is not being said. Market researchers tend to be curious people and it was my sense of curiosity that drew me to the profession in the first place. I have always been fascinated by what people think and how they act, why they buy what they buy, what needs they're trying to fulfill, and what makes them happy, miserable, bored, scared, anxious, loyal, surprised, and delighted. Curiosity was what propelled me to conduct hundreds of interviews and focus groups and to survey tens of thousands of people in my career. I have spent countless hours in peoples' homes, poking around their kitchens and closets. I've gone grocery shopping with them and met their families. I have asked people all over the world about their health, their finances, their perceived purpose in life. I was so busy chasing insights into other people, it had never occurred to me to do the same for myself.

✦

FOR SEVERAL YEARS, on the third Thursday of every month, I have met with a CEO peer group called L3, short for Listen, Learn and Lead. Two years into my business, in 2011, I was invited to apply to the group and was stunned when I was accepted. My company was considerably smaller than everyone else's and I was the lone female. From day one I felt like an imposter. However, over the years, the importance of the group's impact on me and my business was undeniable. As a CEO without a boss or a board to guide me, it was L3 who held me accountable. And it was to these L3 executives that, with some trepidation, I revealed my new goal of seeking insight into myself. Now that my goal was out in the world, I had to do something about it. And this is where Ean comes in.

Early in the morning, two days a week, about twenty of us would drag ourselves into the gym for a two-hour climbing session. A fun, chatty, and driven group, we had become close over the years. Ean, our climbing coach, was our leader—also a third-degree black belt in Kung Fu—and unlike anyone I had ever met. He modelled the qualities that inspired me: strength, dedication, discipline, and determination. Ean also talked about stuff that I didn't understand like visualizing, breathing, and "looking within." At what? I used to think. My bones? My organs? My subcutaneous fat cells?

One morning, a few weeks after the L3 meeting, I overheard Ean talking to a fellow climber about a personal transformation program he was thinking of offering. My ears perked up immediately. Transformation. Now I had a goal, someone to help me with it, and a group of CEOs who would hold me accountable to it. As an achiever this was my sweet spot. What I needed now was structure—and I was already in the possession of the perfect framework.

When market researchers take on a new client project, they follow a certain project structure. Projects tend to last anywhere from four to twelve weeks and have a definitive beginning (a kick-off session), middle (fieldwork, that is conducting surveys, focus groups, and/or interviews), and end (the research report which provides a summary and interpretation of the insights we've discovered as well as outlining the implications of these insights). It made sense for me to apply the project framework to my situation. I would turn the research lens around and focus on myself, using my craft and experience as a vehicle for self-discovery. I decided to call it my *Mesearch* project.[2] Four years later, this book is my final report.

Like most research reports, I've structured the book in three sections. The first part is the background and objectives section where I provide some deeper context for my achiever fever, as well as provide a more detailed explanation of how and why the mesearch project came into being. The second part of the book is the fieldwork—the experiential part of the project. I begin to understand the power of the incessantly nasty, nattering voice in my head. And, as I engage it, I learn more about this inner critic, where it comes from, and how to manage it. I investigate the role that cognitive biases play in decision-making, discover the pervasive power of irrational thinking, and learn why being present is the inflection point. The last part of the book explores the implications of my mesearch and presents the idea that through practice, "letting go" can be the key to curing the classic symptoms of achiever fever while sharpening the ability to accomplish your goals at the same time.

All market research reports have a methodology section, that is, an explanation of how the information and insights were collected. The methodology section typically talks about how many focus groups were conducted or the number of people that were surveyed. As I am the primary source of material, the methodology for this book is a little different. I don't claim to be an expert in anything other than asking questions, and the questions I asked drew me toward disciplines like psychotherapy, neuroscience, behavioural economics, and Buddhism. This book is full of my interpretations of what I've learned from teachers, books, articles, speakers, podcasts, and documentaries on those subjects. For people wishing to undertake their own research, I have included a list of sources and recommended reading at the back of the book.

As I wrote the first draft of this book I was only comfortable writing about my own experience as a mesearcher. But the market researcher in me realized I was missing an important opportunity to connect with other sufferers of achiever fever. That led me to conduct the online survey of self-reported achievers I mentioned previously. The questions were extremely personal (for example, "What does your inner critic say to you?"), and I was gratified to see how open people allowed themselves to be under the promise of anonymity. Almost all of them were suffering from various symptoms of achiever fever.

Among the survey questions, the respondents were asked to fill in the blank to the following statement: "If I'm not achieving, I'm_____." Common responses included: failing, worthless, losing, stagnant, wasting time, lazy, ordinary, worried. Reading their candid replies, I realized I was no different and that I was writing for all achievers who are tired of feeling miserable and who want to change. And I knew that there was a need for this book because I was looking for something like it when I realized I was sick of feeling so terrible. Nothing in the business section at the time appealed to me and I didn't want to venture into the self-help section—way too woo-woo over there. I needed something that hovered between these sections of the bookstore—personal development for the professional. I believe market research as a route to self-discovery goes some way to straddling both sections of the bookstore. This book uses language achievers will relate to. Sure there are also a few hippie-dippie sounding words but nothing kooky. I have a business to run, I can't do kooky.

As I wrapped up the final draft, I also realized that I wrote it because I'm an achiever. Of course, I'd write a book! And yes, writing the book has brought many achiever fever symptoms back, made me feel like a fraud, and given me several nights like the one I wrote about at the beginning of this introduction. But the more I write and share about what I've learned, the better I feel. I feel more connected to myself and more connected to others. And that feels better than any achievement.

Change is more about subtraction than it is addition. Over the past few years, I have shed layers of mental fog and restriction. There is no "new" person, just a stronger, brighter me. I learned how to get out of my own way and what that phrase means. I have learned how to use and practice self-awareness to create a richer, fuller, more connected life. I have learned how to live my life with infinitely more joy and peace than I have ever experienced. I learned how to live purposefully, staying present and observant. I learned how to let go. But, most important of all, I finally woke up from the feverish dream I had lived in for decades. Yes, the fever frequently beckons and it takes effort to keep from slipping back into its grip. But, as an achiever, if there's one thing I do have on my side in that battle it is the ability to put in the work required to halt the fever. In some ways that explains the real reason for writing this book—it is my medicine.

One final note to add—because I would have been thinking this if I picked up this book four years ago: isn't all of this thinking about yourself simply self-absorption? Centuries of writers and philosophers say that self-discovery is the most important thing you could ever do. Aristotle wrote, "Knowing yourself is the beginning of all wisdom." The Hindu sage Ramana Maharshi said, "Your own self-realization is the greatest service you can render the world." Only by understanding yourself can you understand others. Only when you are generous with yourself can you be generous to others. Only when you feel compassion for yourself can you feel compassion for others. And, ultimately, only when you love yourself can you love others. Self-discovery is powerful—it never ends and is the most fulfilling and gratifying work I've ever done.

PART ONE
Objectives

Chapter 1

STRIVING MYSELF CRAZY

When clients hire my company Lux Insights to conduct research, it's because they need market information. A financial institution may ask us to explore the appeal of a new product among millennials or a tech company may ask us to determine the perceived strength of a brand versus their competitors. Rather than launch into surveys and interviews, we first conduct some background research so that we can better understand the context of the situation and ensure that our objectives for the research are clear. It made sense to approach my own research project the same way and relive a little of my own history. But where to start?

When I was about fifteen, I wrote on a cue card: "The point of origin depends on where we think we are now." I must have read it in a book and it seemed very wise, so I copied it down and put it in a shoebox that held my report cards and swimming medals. Twenty-five years later, the words on that cue card were the guidance that I needed. My personal research project began because I was sick of the suffering. Now I needed to look back and find the points in my life at which instances of that sickness had initially cropped up.

A few weeks later I visited a co-worker's house. As their toddler placed books in my lap for me to read, I chatted with my co-worker's wife. I told her how tired I was of pushing myself so hard and how unhappy it was making me. She was a sympathetic ear. She, too, she said, always felt like she was striving. *Striving.* On my drive home, the word reverberating in my head, I recognized that it captured how I felt, like Sisyphus pushing his boulder up a mountain. There seemed to be only one direction in my mindset and that was upwards. This idea of constant striving seemed to sum up the mentally exhausting, confidence-sapping, self-doubt-inducing fever I was aching from by the age of forty-one. I didn't have to go too far back in my life to find a similar situation. Ten years previously, my achiever fever had flared up to the point that I needed medication.

I got divorced when I turned thirty-one. Though the relationship had started in university when I was nineteen, the marriage lasted only a couple of years. Part of the reason the relationship ended was because I decided it was my job to push us both along our career paths. I wanted my husband to be as ambitious as I was, and he wanted me to slow down and enjoy our life. The marriage was doomed and when it ended I doubled down on my striving. I was determined to emerge from the divorce stronger than ever. Soon I was working out twice a day, training hard for the upcoming World Masters Games in swimming, and putting in long hours at work.

At this point in my career, I was working for a global market research company in their Vancouver office and had already been promoted several times. My boss encouraged my ambition and saw that I was ready for bigger challenges. He decided to put me and a co-worker, we'll call him Paul, in charge of developing new business in Seattle. Paul and I worked together to create a pipeline of new US clients for the Vancouver office. Paul was driven, funny, and smart with a knack for analogies. As I watched him pulling in prospective clients with his witty banter, it didn't take me long to start hating him. The fear of being beaten by him amplified the urgency I was already feeling to find new clients, and I stepped up my efforts driving back and forth between Vancouver and Seattle, setting up meetings, and pitching business. Unlike Paul, who was married, I had no one tying me down and within a few months I was spending as much time in Seattle as I was in Vancouver.

My boss saw the potential for a new Seattle office and proposed that I be the one to move down, build a team, and create a new business unit. By this point I had met Chris and was developing feelings for him, but I couldn't say no to this new opportunity. A few months later, my work visa in place, I said good bye to Chris, fired up my playlist, and hit the road. The drive didn't go anything like I had expected. I had pictured myself singing along to my music, surging with energy and happiness, off to start my new life. Instead, I felt like a zombie with nothing but client work circling around in my head. My state probably had something to do with the fact that I hadn't had more than three hours of sleep a night for the past six months.

In my Vancouver home, the bedroom walls were a deep raspberry red. I had them painted that colour post-divorce. Each night I would lie in my bed staring at those walls, willing myself to fall asleep. The worst feeling was when I would hear the seagulls start crying around five in the morning. Once I heard them, I knew there would be no more opportunity for sleep. Soon after the seagulls started, birdsong would float through my window. Something so beautiful, at that time of my life, sounded like harpies from the underworld. And as I gave up on sleep and got out of bed, I felt destined to spend the day in the underworld as well.

Once I made the decision to move to Seattle, my inability to sleep got worse. My mind would run in constant circles about where to live in Seattle. The new office was on the east side, but the west side of the city was where the cool neighbourhoods were located. I agonized incessantly over this decision at night: east side west side, east side west side, and then a glance at the clock. Fuck! 3:15 am already. East side west side, east side west side, east side west side.... Eventually, the cries of the gulls would interrupt my loop of worry. I didn't know whether to feel sick or relieved that the night was over. In hindsight, the decision about where to live felt like the only thing I had some control over. If I chose the east side, my life would go one way. If I chose the west, my life would go another. I made the decision into a far bigger deal than it needed to be, but achiever fever has a tendency to preclude one from rational thinking.

I finally made the decision to move to the west side—it was the location of a swim club that tipped it. The Green Lake Ducks swam at five in the morning, but, I told myself, surely it would be possible to make that time once I got this sleep thing beat. All will fall into place, I said: in bed by nine, asleep by nine-thirty, seven restful hours, and then in the pool at five in the morning with my new fun friends, coffee and newspaper to follow, and a productive day at work. In reality, I only made it to that work-out a handful of times. In fact, after a few weeks of moving to Seattle, the swimming and exercise stopped entirely due to my complete inability to sleep.

Meanwhile, in the new Seattle office, I was winning new cli-ents, hiring new staff, and building what would soon become one of the fastest-growing business units in the North Ameri-can arm of the company. I led with enthusiasm, feeding off the praise of my boss back in Vancouver. My team grew to ten; I designed retreats to tighten our culture and we became like family. I found out later that none of them had any idea how troubled I was.

The faster we grew, the worse my sleep got. I spent hours alternating between being worried about losing a client and being disgusted with myself for not being able to do what seemed to come so naturally to everyone else in the world: sleep. As the months progressed, I began to develop a fantasy of being in a car accident that would not cause any physical damage to myself or my car, but instead would put me in the hospital either in a coma or in a state where the doctors would have to feed me full of drugs. Either way I would sleep blissfully for days. Then, when I awoke, happy and refreshed, someone would be there to take care of me—my family, Chris, my team, anyone. I wouldn't feel weak, because this car accident was not my fault—I had no control over what happened.

Of course, as sleep deprived as I was, it didn't take long to have an actual car accident. I was driving around West Seattle trying to find a car insurance office. This was in the days before Google Maps and I had printed out the driving instructions on a piece of paper and left it on my passenger seat. Leaning over to read the directions while driving, it was easy to make a wrong turn. Realizing I was about to drive in the wrong direction, I decided to backtrack by reversing through a U-turn. In doing so, I backed into a sage green–coloured luxury car.

It wasn't a crash, but it was enough of an impact that I knew damage had been caused and that it was my fault. I couldn't contain my shame and I put my head down on my steering wheel and sobbed. An older gentleman soon tapped at my window and, through my tears, I babbled something about having recently moved to the city and being lost in an area I hadn't been in before. The man took down my information and asked if he could call anyone for me. I sniffled that I would be OK and we parted ways.

I drove home (there was no damage to my car, at least that part of the car accident fantasy had worked) and got into the bath. I remember thinking, as I lay in the tub, that this must be the point where people starting thinking about turning to drink, drugs, or Jesus. I had a palpable feeling in my chest that I could only describe as rot. I may have looked perfectly normal on the outside, but I felt like I was rotting from the inside. The fever was in my bones.

A month later, the doorbell of my apartment rang. A man stood on the doorstep holding a large box with a bakery name embossed on it that was addressed to me. I thanked him and took it inside. I opened the box to find two dozen flower-shaped sugar cookies, iced in pink and yellow. There was a note inside which read: "I'm sorry your moving experience has been hard. I hope you're feeling better. Welcome to Seattle." The box of cookies was from the man whose car I'd backed into. I was overwhelmed with an emotion I wasn't familiar with. I felt seen—someone had seen the truth of my suffering and had acknowledged the pain I was feeling. His act of kindness pierced my grey clouds for a few seconds only, but it was long enough for me to wake up and admit defeat. I needed help.

The receptionist at the doctor's office gave me a questionnaire to fill out—I had to check off anything that was happening in my life at that moment. I checked off the boxes beside "move," "new job," and "divorce," a first-world anxiety triumvirate. There was another box my pen hovered over: "passive suicidal thoughts." The car accident fantasy was the good kind. I wasn't ready to acknowledge that I had had much worse. I walked out of the office with a prescription and a referral to a therapist. My therapist, who I saw for a year on a weekly basis, told me I was experiencing a mix of anxiety and depression; they were feeding each other and thus responsible for my insomnia. I remember feeling mixed emotions hearing her diagnosis: relief that there was something wrong with me and shame that I was a bad person, that I couldn't cope, that I was weak. The worst of it was having to tell my family. I was the oldest of three sisters and had always strived to model success. Now I was asking my little sister, a doctor, for advice on antidepressants. And Chris, who had been driving down to see me every second or third weekend, patiently tried to reassure me all would be well many a time.

After trying a few different drugs at different doses, we hit on the right combination. I knew it was working when I caught myself singing along to the radio in my car. My sleep came back, my worrying calmed down, and I threw myself into work and fitness activities again. My energy surged, business kicked into high gear, and my team blew away our targets. The company rewarded my team with an all-expenses paid trip, including significant others, to Scottsdale, Arizona. One night at dinner I made a speech telling everyone how thrilled I was by our accomplishments. And I felt the thrill, too, especially after a few glasses of wine. I had built a thriving business, learned to hire and fire, developed an enviable business culture, and was the public face of it all.

Still, I was hiding my suffering from the team in Seattle—it was never a topic of discussion, ever. According to my achiever survey, many high achievers are intimately familiar with insomnia, anxiety, and depression, and, like me, they rarely discuss these conditions with anyone else. And I was surprised by what the survey revealed about how common these conditions are. More than a third of the respondents reported experiencing insomnia or poor sleep in the week prior to filling out the survey, with a total of just over fifty percent experiencing it in the past month. When it comes to anxiety (which was phrased in the survey as not necessarily clinically diagnosed but strong enough that you can tell it is affecting you), just over a quarter had experienced it in the last week with almost fifty percent in the last month. One quarter of the survey respondents had experienced depression in the past month with a total of just over forty percent in the past six months. It wasn't just me who endured sleepless nights, riddled with worry and anxiety, using whatever crutch—alcohol, food, exercise, work—it took to cope.

To this day, I am grateful that medication gave me a reset. I did not have the tools to change my perspective on my own. When I look back on that period of my life now, I can see how close I was to learning some important things about myself. Instead, the medication papered over a hole that would reveal itself again in my early forties. Though the antidepressants had helped me calm down and sleep, they did nothing for my achiever fever. Within six months of being on medication, my goal was to get off it. I didn't want to have to take something to make me "better." I had to prove to myself that I could sleep well and live life minus anxiety, depression, and worry, without the aid of medication.

✦

IN 2008, THREE years after moving to Seattle, the business flourishing, I quit the company. This had always been my plan. When I had moved down, with six years at the company already under my belt, I knew I only wanted to work a few more. My belief at this stage of my career was that ten years was too long to be at any one company. Plus, as I built the business for this global firm, it had occurred to me that I might be able to do this for myself. So, I set a new goal—to travel the world. This trip would be a great way to spend some serious time with Chris; it would get me out of my non-compete agreement and help wean me off the medication.

We ended up following the sun for sixteen months. First we drove up to Alaska and the Yukon in Chris's camper van for the summer. Then we went backpacking for two months in Australia, two months in New Zealand, took a quick trip to the South Pacific, travelled through South East Asia for a few months, and finally we spent a summer in France. We spent time in thirteen countries exploring, hiking, climbing, swimming, and diving. When I wasn't moving, I was reading, picking up books in second hand stores and hostels. I read over eighty books that year.

It was the first time as an adult that I didn't have either school or career as my guiding light. I stopped taking any medication and was sleeping soundly. But, just like Alain de Botton describes in *The Art of Travel*, I had also packed myself and my idiosyncratic tendency to goal-set along with my backpack.

Rather than enjoy each day as it came, it only took me a couple of weeks to decide I needed a purpose for this trip.

My new goal became beating the budget that Chris and I had set for the trip. I tracked our spending down to the penny, made pie charts illustrating our finances, and kept careful notes of who paid for what. In an Alaskan Safeway, I told Chris he couldn't buy the peanut butter he wanted because it was fifty cents more than the cheaper brand. (He bought the peanut butter after telling me that I either needed to calm down or travel on my own.) I also decided I would use this trip to improve my fitness and I chose most of our hikes based on their difficulty level. To keep my brain sharp, I spent hours writing reviews of all my books and blogging about our adventures. I was also constantly planning: Where would we go next? Where would we stay? What should we see? What should we hike? On our long multi-day hiking trips, I would run scenarios in my head of what I would do with my career when I got back. Just like the east side/west side conversation that had spun in circles through my brain when I moved to Seattle, I hiked to the rhythm of should I or shouldn't I start my own business.

Our last three months of the trip were spent in a 400-square-foot apartment in Chamonix, a small town located at the base of Mont Blanc, nestled on the borders of Italy, Switzerland, and France. It was as idyllic as it sounds. Most days we would pack a lunch fresh from the farmers' market and venture off on a climbing, hiking, or biking adventure, or swim with the Chamonix masters swim group. Other days, we would laze in cafes, reading and drinking coffee, and cook. I was even doing cross-stitch. By this point in the trip, I had finally learned to relax and was fully enjoying myself. But we had set a budget for our travels and our bank accounts signalled it was time to go home. On the flight back, Chris and I ran the numbers and realized we needed to make half of what we made before the trip to cover our basic needs, save a little bit, and still afford a few luxuries like a monthly house cleaner. After sixteen months of living out of backpacks, we vowed not to get sucked back into the rat race.

That vow lasted three months. There's nothing like starting a business to kick the striving into high gear.

Within a month of landing in Vancouver, I called a few of my old clients and asked them if they would be interested in working with me if I set up my own shop. They encouraged me to do it, and now that I had put the idea out there, I had to follow through. First, I had to decide on a name before I could incorporate. I spent days trying to come up with something but I couldn't find anything that I liked or that wasn't already taken. Working with my favourite branding team, we came up with the name together: Lux Insights. Lux is the Latin word for "light," and that is what research does—it sheds light on the subject in question. It was easy to spell and easy to say. What I didn't know at the time was that it was the perfect name as it contained the seed for what I would be doing eight years later—looking for the "lux" within.

Next I developed a business plan and worked with a designer to create a logo and a website. During those first few weeks I remember dragging myself to my desk in the morning to make calls to prospective clients and work on my business plan. With one eye on the clock I would look forward to the time when I could knock off and have a glass of wine. The feeling that filled me every day was the sense that I was playing a role, that I was simply an actor, and that the business would never work. I told myself that I'd try it for six months and then go and get a real job.

My first client, a restaurant chain, referred by a swimming friend, arrived on my doorstep within the first two months. I had been missing the camaraderie of working in an office, and thankfully, the client wanted me to work out of their offices a couple of days a week. A health care client came onboard next and then an insurance client, which meant I had enough work to merit hiring my first employee.

The first hire was the toughest because it doubled my need to succeed and the subsequent anxiety that tagged along with that need. Lux wasn't just me anymore, I had someone else to be responsible for, and I had to be accountable. My first hire was Hanson Lok, a sharp, hard-working, caring, and dedicated co-worker of mine in Seattle. He had moved down a year after me to help fulfill the business that was flowing in and he moved back to Vancouver around the same time I had left to travel the world. I remember pitching him at a local coffee shop with zero expectation that he would say yes. I was asking him to leave one of the world's largest research companies to come and work with me, a year-old market research agency with all of three clients. "What took you so long?" he asked. I had my first employee.

The business grew quickly and became the focus of my life. Terrified of the mounting expenses, I had to take on all the business functions I had never touched at my previous company— the bookkeeping, marketing, HR. I took note of when Hanson fed his dog filtered water from our water dispenser and made my disapproval known. He rolled his eyes.

A company was the perfect outlet for my need for growth and success. After all, what do you do with a company other than grow it? As I saw the increase in revenue from year one to year two and again in year three, growth became my guiding force. I started reading *Entrepreneur* and fixated on how fast so many of the profiled companies were growing. I quickly lost sight of the fact that I was running a small professional services company and started comparing my company to the Silicon Valley companies described in these magazines. As I talked about my goals with other business owners, I would draw a hockey stick shape with my palm signifying my expectations for success. And, relatively speaking, Lux was successful right out of the gate. It was profitable by its second year and maintained that profitability as I expanded it, adding new employees each year.

But, as a small business owner, and following all the advice in those industry magazine articles, I never let myself get comfortable. And indeed, in a professional services business, it is very difficult to predict success outside of three months. The days of long-term anchor clients have passed. My first large client, the insurance company, went from about eighty percent of my business in the first couple of years to less than twenty percent in year three. There were constant business threats: political elections, clients moving companies, new competitors, as well as all the potential threats I would worry about at night: employees leaving, workplace injury claims—the magazines were right. There was no comfort to be had.

In the early days, my aunt once asked me if I spent more time working now that I had my own company. At that point, I had a few employees and was proud to say that no, I didn't. I was good at delegating work and I was actually spending fewer hours working than I had at my previous company. Then she asked how much time did I spend thinking about my company? Without hesitation, I answered ninety-five percent. I was obsessed with my company, obsessed with growing it, obsessed with proving I was a good business person.

Within a couple of years, I had lost myself. By equating my

personal success with my company's success, I became the company. My new identity was "business owner." It was a rare occasion when I congratulated myself because I had to stay on guard. A loss could turn me inside out. Occasionally, a competitor would win a project over us, or we lost an account because our client contact was replaced, or we didn't make it to the table to bid on a project in the first place. I always assumed these losses were my fault—I hadn't tried hard enough. I hadn't prepared properly. I wasn't reading the right business books. I wasn't asking enough of my employees. When these losses happened, I would often find myself in a downward spiral, my thoughts a tornado of despair.

In these situations, sports distracted me. I'd get myself back on track for a few weeks by ascending a tough climbing route or swimming a personal best. But, more often, when something didn't go according to plan, I'd get into what Chris termed "a funk." Sometimes they lasted a few hours, sometimes a few days. Worst of all, these funks would keep me awake at night, filling me with fear that I was going to fail, that I didn't have what it took, that I was still that actor playing a role, and everyone would find out that I didn't know what I was doing.

And there I was, at the age of forty-one, five years into creating a profitable, successful business, wanting so badly to feel energized, enthused, and proud. But I was in the grip of achiever fever and again facing the misery I had doctored with medication almost ten years earlier in 2005. I knew what came next if I didn't take action.

✦

TYPICAL MARKET RESEARCH reports only provide about a half a page of background information because clients are impatient to find out what the research findings show. I was as impatient when writing this book, wanting to share what I've learned. But it's useful to spend some time considering what motivates high achievers in the first place. And that is exactly what I asked the respondents in my survey: What motivates you to be an achiever? Why is achieving so important to you? This type of question is called "open-ended," meaning that the responses are text-based. Survey respondents can write as little or as much as they like in response to these kinds of questions, and it is the researcher's job to read through the responses and group them into categories. Here is my interpretation of the key thematic categories in answer to my question:

- Recognition and approval (from parents, bosses, peers, one's children)
- Fear of being left behind (by peers and/or siblings)
- Building a sense of self-worth (if I'm not achieving, I'm nothing)
- Differentiating oneself from the perceived average or ordinary
- Proving to others they can count on us
- Fulfilling a sense of innate potential
- The thrill of accomplishment especially when tied to overcoming self-doubt
- Financial independence and security

Many of these themes struck a chord with my own life experience, but some of them more deeply than the rest.

Several achievers wrote about wanting to meet their parents' high expectations, especially if their parents had suffered hardships to give their kids a better life or if one, or both parents, was a high achiever themselves. This brings to mind a cartoon I once saw that showed a "gone fishing" type sign on a psychologist's door. The sign said, "Talk to your parents."

My father was an engineer who owned his own business while my mother stayed at home until I was twelve, when she went back to school to become an accountant. They were strict and made sure I studied hard but never expressly pushed or pressured me to excel. I was not rewarded for marks, nor did I get in trouble if I didn't do well. Instead, it was my parents' work ethic, and their expectation that we would work hard that had the most impact on me and my two sisters. In and out of the home, my parents always seemed to give everything their full effort, whether it was my father building his business or my mother studying fastidiously for her accounting exams. Rarely did I see them take a break, and even to this day, I will feel guilty sometimes if I find myself sitting on the couch on a Saturday afternoon.

Throughout my childhood, I would often hear one of my father's favourite phrases, "take the initiative." As immigrants from Britain, my parents had shown serious initiative leaving their families to move to Canada in their twenties. That phrase would become my personal tagline as I became an adult. In my early forties, I was still calling home trying to show my dad how I had taken the initiative in whatever it was that I was working on.

The desire to fulfill one's innate potential was a repeated theme in my survey results. According to the survey, more than seven in ten achievers say they fear not living up to their true potential (this feeling is stronger among female respondents than it is for male respondents). One belief that has fired up my achiever fever over the years is that I saw wasted potential as the lowest form of misery. The upshot of this is that I tend to gravitate to activities that I'm good at because it seems easier to reach my potential. However, this means I overlook the fact that potential is amorphous and unlimited. Instead, I strive to fill a seemingly preordained space within me.

Climbing was a good fit for my need to fulfill potential because it involves a finite goal: lead climb the route cleanly (no falling). If I finished it, I succeeded in fulfilling my potential for that route. That kind of thinking often led me into a toxic stew of anger and self doubt. Take the following scenario, for example.

I'm in Red Rocks, a climbing area just outside of Las Vegas. On a narrow rock ledge, I pause and shake my hands out. I can feel my toes cramping inside my shoes, my legs starting to quiver. The next hold is a tiny crimp, a finger-width rock ledge, just below the next bolt. I have to grab that crimp with one hand and clip my quick draw with the other, moving my feet up the wall at the same time. I take a deep breath and lunge for it. Thank God, I catch the ledge with my right hand, bracing one foot against the wall. I'm breathing hard and I'm clinging to that crimp. Now to clip the rope in. I can feel the sweat on my fingers loosening my grip but I hang on, fingertips grating. With my left hand, I grab a draw off my harness and get it on the bolt. Almost safe, my breath now shallow, my legs like sewing machines, I yank the rope up from my harness, reach my shaking hand up to the draw… and fall. It's a fifteen-foot fall, by no means a whipper, but it's enough to feel a surge of fear quickly followed by anger and frustration. I slam my fist against the wall and internally scream, GODDAMNIT! I'm better than this!

Sometimes this anger would fuel the next attempt and I'd get the move. Sometimes I'd yell for my belayer to lower me down. In either instance, my belief was that I had not lived up to my potential.

This kind of self-sabotaging behaviour connects with the belief that many achievers have about the constant need to prove their value. Eighty percent of the achievers in the survey agreed they feel a strong need to prove themselves (again this is higher among women than men). In third year university, two of my professors told me that I could have a career in academics. This was probably the first career-oriented praise I had received and it came at a time when I was starting to wonder what came after university. I leapt at the opportunity to prove them right, completed a master's degree and then won a full fellowship to do a PhD. However, in the process of proving to those professors that I could have an academic career, I tried to do all the required coursework in the first year of my doctorate and burned out.

Perhaps the most potent and sobering theme behind what motivates achievers is this: the addictive feeling of the payoff. It was no surprise to me that more than fifty percent of my surveyed achievers say they are addicted to achieving. Many achievers wrote about how good it feels to accomplish something, especially when they have worked especially hard or overcome self-doubt.

When I signed up to race a 200 fly at a Masters swim meet (swimming butterfly stroke for four lengths of a fifty-metre pool), I had never swum the distance in practice, let alone race it. But fly was my strongest stroke. The coach encouraged me, which, of course, was like catnip—if he believed I could do it I wanted to prove him right. I also knew that I could set myself apart from my swim mates with this achievement as the 200 fly is one of the hardest events to swim. As I trained, I had to contend with the distinct possibility of failure. But since I had already committed, I wasn't about to back down. Four months later, as I swam the last fifty metres of the race, my arms burning with lactic acid, I knew I would finish. When I touched the wall, I was so overwhelmed with pride that I had to duck down under water to hide my tears. The high lasted all evening, but, as I lay in bed that night, I was already thinking about my next swimming goal.

Whatever the reason, the need to achieve keeps us forever striving. Striving to do better in our jobs, get promotions, make more money. Win awards. Buy a bigger house. Buy any house. Buy more houses. Eat less. Work out more. Do more volunteering. Do any volunteering. Be a better mother, father, friend, wife, or husband. Be more organized. Take more holidays. Be more relaxed. Better, more, try, improve, do.

At forty-one, recognizing that I was striving myself crazy, I hit the pause button. I was sick of trying to prove myself, sick of trying to fulfill whatever this thing called potential was, sick of trying to set myself apart. I was exhausted, anxious, and unhappy. I wanted to excel, but not at the expense of my mental health. There had to be a better way.

Chapter 2

CONFESSION

IN LATE 2014, when I finally became aware that my striving was making me crazy, all I knew was that I was aware of feeling sick. I didn't know what action to take or who to talk to about it. Knowing what I know now—that simply being aware can often point us in the right direction—it's not surprising that my next steps seemed to fall into place. Three things transpired between the recognition of my achiever fever and the beginning of my mesearch project—I think of them as stepping stones. The first stone was, of all things, a Jerry Seinfeld show. The second was a confession to L3, my CEO group. And the third was a fateful moment of eavesdropping on my climbing coach, Ean Kramer.

Buying tickets to see Jerry Seinfeld at Caesars Palace was a last-minute decision. Chris and I were in Vegas with a group of climbing friends for his fortieth birthday and, looking for a break from climbing, we decided to go to a show. Although

Chris had seen every *Seinfeld* episode, I'd never been a fan, so he had to talk me into going.

Jerry was brilliant. I had to hold my stomach I was laughing so hard, loving his stories and jokes, each one better than the last. I was stunned by his talent. As I stood up at the end of the show to join in the standing ovation, I looked around and saw that the audience had felt the same way I had: we had just witnessed a master at work. I had an overwhelming feeling of connection to everyone in that theatre.

The real magic, though, was a thought that struck me as I walked down the aisle towards the stairs. As I wiped the tears out of my eyes, it occurred to me that the reason Seinfeld was so funny was because he had an ability to tap into the audience's commonly held thoughts and behaviours that we were either unaware of or that we kept hidden. He had the knack of revealing us to ourselves. Our laughter comes from the surprise and recognition that he has captured us perfectly: "that's exactly what I do/say/think!" we say with delight. My curiosity about the comedian's ability for almost surgical insight stayed with me, and soon I was reading books about comedy, watching hours of comedy specials, attending live comedy shows, and even interviewing local comedians. I asked them about their research process, how they wrote, where they got their material from, and what they thought about the connection between their comedy and the human condition.[3]

The first thing that surprised me was that most of my interviewees described themselves as introverted, anxious, and nervous. Many told a similar story: they were shy kids who one day made someone laugh and, realizing this made them feel good, wanted more. They described the feeling of being on stage as a "high" and they would look for material to feed their addiction.

Off stage, they went back to being the introvert. But being quiet made them more receptive to material—they would look for instances of cognitive dissonance, things that didn't make sense but were accepted as normal. They would listen in on conversations in coffee shops, watch people on subways, and hear and see things the rest of us wouldn't. They honed their powers of observation, becoming more keenly aware of the world around them and more keenly aware of themselves.

When asked who they thought was the most insightful comedian, many gave the same response: Louis C.K. He was also my favourite comedian at the time, though I recognize his recent personal transgressions are grave and must be taken seriously. Then, at the height of his career, Louis C.K had recently sold out Madison Square Garden four nights in a row and was revered as a comedic genius. I encouraged my interviewees to help me understand what made him so good. One comedian succinctly explained it like this: "Louis C.K. has the conversations we have in our head, out loud."[4]

I knew she was right. Louis C.K.'s jokes are about things we can all relate to, from malfunctioning technology to existential angst. But now I saw something that I hadn't quite understood with Seinfeld. Comedians reach deep within themselves to find the insights they weave through their comedy. They must trust that enough of us are going to be able to relate to their truths. But their real power is in their willingness to make themselves vulnerable and share what they've found. I needed to do the same thing if I wanted to change how I felt: I needed to say what was inside me, out loud.

The next stepping stone presented itself in the form of an audience with my monthly CEO peer group, L3. Joining L3 offered more than a powerful networking opportunity for me.

As a business owner with no boss, I knew that I would push myself harder if I had someone holding me accountable. I had mentioned this to my first client, Yuri Fulmer, who subsequently invited me to audition for this CEO group he facilitated. L3 members meet one day a month to talk about their businesses as well as the challenges they don't want to share with their board or employees. I didn't need to be asked twice. At the time, my business was only in its second year, and this was a major opportunity to grow my skills.

My excitement waned when I got online and read about the other members. Most were running multi-million-dollar companies that dwarfed the revenue of my small business. But retreat was not an option. I prepared my PowerPoint presentation, pulling my charts together to show my comparatively modest revenue stream and profitability numbers alongside slides describing the size of the market and my competitors. My legs were shaking when I stood up to present and, after I finished the presentation, I was convinced my company would never be big enough to join such an esteemed group.

They saw it differently. They told me my passion and ambition was obvious and invited me into the group. I was their first female member, and I had the smallest company by far. L3 members soon became my sounding board, my cheerleaders, and my coaches. Meeting for a full day, once a month, the members of L3 gave me the accountability I needed. They also changed the filter I used to view the success of my company. These guys were all about acquisitions, governance, succession planning, equity events, and debt servicing, among other business functions that I didn't understand.

From day one I felt like an imposter. Each month, I would give myself a pep talk before our meetings. I would go in feeling brave and ready to contribute if it killed me. I would try to listen carefully but it wasn't long before the conversation moved into topics with which I had no experience. Inevitably, by the end of the morning, I would usually be beating myself up: Why are you here? You've got nothing to contribute! By mid-afternoon, I would be planning how to get out of the group, and, by the end of the day, I'd be in total despair. But I continued to go back, month after month, because I was learning so much and my business was growing as a result.

In the fall of 2014, Yuri was planning the group's annual retreat to be held in Newport Beach, California. Usually we are given some sort of homework exercise for these retreats and, this time, the exercise was "Your Secret Goal." Yuri told us we needed to come prepared to share the thing we most wanted to accomplish but felt the need to keep secret.

As soon as the exercise was announced, my goal was there in my head: get rid of my self-doubt, be more confident, and get out of my own way. The thought of saying this out loud in front of a group of accomplished business peers was terrifying. I tried to come up with other secret goals, but I now knew from my exploration of the comedian's world that the power of vulnerability was immensely liberating—I had to do it.

Newport Beach is a very wealthy town: private jets at the airport, a high-end sports car dealership across the street from our resort hotel, yachts parked up and down the marina. The L3 group met for breakfast in a room overlooking the ocean. It was a typical hotel meeting room with a projector and flip chart and a continental breakfast laid out on the side table. We kicked off the retreat as we do all our meetings with something called Significant Events. Each member has eight minutes to share what's going on in their work and personal life, no interruptions allowed. As I've gotten to know these guys, I've become invested in their stories. However, whenever it was my turn to share, I would get nervous and feel an overwhelming need to prove that they had made a good choice in bringing me into the group. Imposter syndrome engulfed me every time I had to present my Significant Events. Were they significant enough?

After the Significant Events portion, it was time to replenish our coffee. The food and beverage manager came into the room, looked around, and made a beeline for me. "Is everything going well ma'am? Anything your group needs?" Bemused, the men left at the table looked at me wondering how I was going to handle the assumption that I was the event coordinator. Inwardly I sighed, then pointed to Yuri and said, "Ask the person in charge."

Following the coffee break, it was time for the Secret Goal exercise. We moved the meeting to the adjoining outside terrace as it was starting to warm up. I could see workers scrubbing the yachts, seniors in tennis whites pushing little dogs in strollers. Yuri called the meeting back to order and explained the Secret Goal again. This was our opportunity to share something in confidence, among peers we trusted, something we aspired to but were reticent to talk about for whatever reason. It was still cool in the morning air, and I could feel myself shivering because I was wearing a sleeveless dress. I was also shivering because it was time for the reveal. A week previous I had written my thoughts down in a gust of confidence but now I was panicking. I frantically searched my brain, looking for another secret goal, anything!

The first person to share made a statement that only increased my fear. "My secret goal" he said, "is to one day... walk on the moon." What? Seriously? My mind spun around trying to come up with a significantly less personal goal. We moved onto the next member. "My secret goal," he said, "is to play the piano in my house." Someone wanted to be a painter. Someone wanted an expensive car. I was freaking out; my mind was blank. Was this how the exercise was going to go? Then it was my turn. I was more than shivering, I was shaking. All I could do was blurt it out, hearing my voice break as it floated over the table, "My secret goal is that I want to be a more confident person. I want to get rid of my self-doubt. I want to get out of my own way. I'm sick of feeling worried and anxious all the time and I don't want to feel this way anymore."

The table was quiet. In the comedy world, this is where the payoff happens. I don't know what I was expecting, maybe someone to exclaim, "Claire, you've always been so confident! I can't believe you really feel like this!" I suddenly felt the same way I did when climbing a challenging route—exposed and scared. The imposter had been revealed. Then someone said, "It took a lot of confidence to say that," and suddenly everyone was nodding their head and agreeing. I stared at them blankly, too addled to say anything else, and we moved on to the next person.

I didn't understand it at the time, but in speaking my truth, I had begun the process of getting out of my own way. Though my ego was screaming at me to hide my weakness, something else inside me overrode it and decided to go in a different direction. It was early days, but I was beginning to wake up from my feverish dream.

After the retreat's Secret Goal exercise, all I could feel was a sense of awkward discomfort. The other members continued to treat me as they always did, joking around, asking questions about my company and my partner Chris, but no one acknowledged what I had said. I was keyed up, anxious, and as the day progressed, increasingly disgusted with myself. What kind of businessperson was I to talk about "feelings" at a retreat like this? All I had to do was get through a few more hours, and then I could have a glass of wine and move the anxiety down from my chest and into my stomach where I could bury it.

At the end of the meeting, back on the patio, I had a glass of wine, then another, then another. Only then did I start to settle down. Later that evening, one of the members approached me, privately. He told me he thought my goal was a powerful one. "Do you realize," he said, "what kind of confidence it took to admit that in the first place?"

Late that night, I took the elevator up to my floor with another member. As we walked down the hall together he said to me, "I want you to know how impressed I was by what you said today. Deep down, that's a goal of mine too. Thank you for saying what you did."

Maybe it was the wine, but at that moment, I thought I understood something that comedians do. By sharing their truth publicly, they can light a spark. Maybe I had lit something in another member but, most importantly, I had lit something in myself. I went to bed that night, certainly a little drunk, but also with the knowledge that now my secret was out, I had to do something about it. I had joined L3 because I was looking for accountability. Now I had to figure out exactly how I was going to get rid of my achiever fever.

✦

You know that saying, when you're ready, the teacher will appear? That's what happened next. My third stepping stone

THE ACHIEVER FEVER CURE

was Ean Kramer, my climbing coach. Before I met Ean, I had climbed for years but had never "trained" for climbing. When I got back from my round-the-world trip, I saw an ad for a climbing group class called "Roosters" because it was held on Wednesday and Friday mornings at six. Chris and I decided to sign up.

The sessions were two hours long and we climbed in pairs for the first ninety minutes and then did circuit training for the last half hour. By the end of the first session I was utterly spent, my muscles ached, and I was nauseous from cardio components like tuck jumps and stair sprints. Of course, I was hooked.

Ean led our group. As we climbed, he would offer advice on which route to try, how to set up for a particularly tough move, or simply provide encouragement. "Keep breathing!" he would say as we struggled through a route, "you're stronger than you think!" I had no idea how important those words would come to be.

Ean coached us on our climbing abilities, but it was less about working the grades and more about moving our bodies. This was new for a lot of us, certainly me. Getting to know how my body moved in space, feeling the balance in my feet, noticing when my arms were locking up because they were bent—this was the type of feedback he gave us. It was less a case of powering through the moves and more about climbing intentionally by visualizing the route, breathing purposefully throughout, and moving fluidly using good technique. And it worked. We all became much stronger climbers.

The Roosters program was offered September through May with the summers off, as most of us wanted to climb outside. One summer, though, we asked Ean if he could design a four-month program to keep our fitness levels up. He rented some space in a community centre and about ten of us signed up. Working outside the climbing gym gave Ean an opportunity to throw in some martial arts exercises as well. We'd leave the classes with aches in muscles we didn't even know we had.

But it was also in these classes that we saw a different side of Ean. He would have us start the class with our eyes closed, just breathing. Both Chris and I were impatient to get to the training but we went along with it. At the end of the class, he would have us close our eyes again and talk us through an exercise that sounded like this: "Smile at your toes, your feet, your ankles. Now smile at your shins, your knees, your thighs, your hips." It went on until we were "smiling" at our liver, spleen, parts of our brain, even at our eyes. It was only a couple of minutes, but driving home, Chris and I would make fun of this crazy exercise. We'd send each other emails later in the day, signing off with "don't forget to smile at your butt!" But though we joked about Ean's odd teaching methods, we were smitten with him because he'd made us all so strong.

Not long after the Secret Goal experience with the L3 group, I overheard Ean talking to a fellow climber about a program he was thinking of launching. I started eavesdropping. (I'm a researcher—I eavesdrop all the time.) He called it a personal transformation program where he would work with people who wanted to change themselves—people who wanted to lose weight or people who were feeling stuck in a rut. Under my breath I mumbled, "God, what I wouldn't give to transform myself. Sign me up." In a life-changing moment, Ean heard me.

At the end of class, he came over and asked me what I was interested in changing. "Everything." I said. The floodgates opened and I told him how unhappy I was. How I felt stressed, anxious, and worried all the time. How I was addicted to thinking about my business, how my sleep was messed up. How I was full of self-doubt and insecurity. How I was so desperate to get out of my own way. He locked eyes with me and said, "If you really want to change, I can help you."

"Yes!" I cried, "Yes, I want to change! I'm so sick of feeling this way!"

"OK," he replied, "Meet me for coffee next week and we'll talk about it."

I left the gym feeling elated. Finally! Finally, I was going to take control and fix myself!

The giddiness quickly turned to worry on the drive home. Personal transformation? What the hell was that? Was this going to be super weird, and I would have to smile at my bones? Worry turned to fear and I felt sick. What was I getting myself into? I calmed myself down by thinking that (a) I could always back out, (b) I did want to change and I should at least hear him out, and, (c) if nothing else, I could report back to L3 that I had tried something.

Three days later, in late fall of 2014, Ean and I met at a vegan coffee shop close to my office, which only heightened my nervousness because the location was full of weird, to me at least, hippie vibes. He asked me to repeat all the things I wanted to change—physically and mentally. It was easy to start with the physical. I wanted to climb stronger. I wanted to climb without fear. I wanted to fit into a couple of dresses that had gotten tight. Then I told him I wanted to grow my business and be a good leader. But most of all, I said, I wanted to feel confident, get rid of my self-doubt, and get out of my own way. I was sick of feeling so miserable and I wanted to enjoy my life.

Ean told me that the program would be intensive and that we would be meeting three times a week. One of those sessions would be a one-on-one, hour-long, in-person session. We could do it at my house, a coffee shop, or wherever was convenient for me. There was no agenda for this session; we could talk about, or do, whatever I felt like. Another of those three sessions would be an hour-long personal training session. The third session I could choose from one of the several two-hour martial arts classes that he taught: Kung Fu, Tai Chi, or Neigong. (I chose Kung Fu because it sounded tougher.) If I missed a session, I could make it up some time over the next couple of weeks, but it was understood that with my travel schedule, sessions would be missed. He wasn't too concerned. He said that he'd give me things to do outside of the session that I could do on my own.

The full program was a year long, but we agreed to start with four months and then re-evaluate. He said he would put together a contract, noting everything we'd discussed that day, and would be ready to start early in the new year. As I walked out of the coffee shop, I was shaking with excitement. I'd one day be brimming with energy and enthusiasm, running my business with complete confidence and be the fittest I'd ever been? Sign me up!

It took no more than five minutes after our meeting had ended for me to start second guessing myself. I'd have to tell Chris about this scary-sounding "commitment," and Chris would think I'd hired the dreaded "life coach" (code for "you can't get your shit together so pay a bunch of money to someone else who can't get their shit together."). My sisters would roll their eyes at me behind my back and discuss their disbelief that I had to hire someone because I couldn't figure out how to live my life. I was already convinced my parents thought I was too self-involved and this would just strengthen that perception. And the time commitment! At least one of those three sessions would have to happen during the workday. Surely my employees would question my commitment to Lux and my work ethic. And Kung Fu? Was I Keanu Reeves? This was ridiculous! I got home that day thinking I'd rather just walk away from the whole thing.

But that evening, after I told Chris about my meeting with Ean, he said this: "Claire, you and I have been together for ten years. I've seen you go through a lot of funks. It's not super easy, you know, trying to get you get out of your doom and gloom. If Ean says he can help you, he's probably right. And Kung Fu sounds cool. You're gonna end up kicking my ass. And maybe you'll have to smile at your bones a little, but what the hell, I say go for it."

Once he'd said this, I knew he'd be disappointed if I backed out. Plus, there was a business case for all this. If working with Ean meant that my business would grow, what was the harm in trying? But I had never done anything quite like this before and I didn't know how to categorize it in my brain.

Ean normalized it before I could. The next week, he presented me with a summary of what we discussed in the coffee shop. At the top of the page, he had written the word "objectives." And that's the moment when I decided to make the entire exercise into a research project. Like how my company's projects reveal insights for clients, this program was going to reveal insights about me. Now that I could label it, it felt slightly less peculiar. And by thinking of it as a research project, I was in familiar territory.

I looked at the list of objectives Ean had written down:

- Banish self-doubt
- Build confidence
- Enjoy taking calculated risks
- Be a better, more decisive leader

- Be happy with herself when she accomplishes something
- Stop comparing herself to others
- Strengthen overall motivation and focus
- Be able to maintain a relaxed state, particularly in groups of people
- Minimize anxiety in order to experience greater peace
- Love her body instead of judging it
- Lean up in order to fit into older clothes
- Feel and be more limber
- Be a stronger climber
- Eat a healthier, wider variety of foods
- Cut back on alcohol (no longer have the need for alcohol to de-stress)

I was ecstatic—this was exactly what I was looking for! But there was more. Ean had also listed some objectives we hadn't discussed:

Ean will teach Claire:
- How to centre herself
- How to control her mind and body
- How to have greater awareness
- How to become stronger
- How to shift her emotional state
- How to release stress in a positive way
- How to overcome/break through obstacles
- How to have thoughts, speech, and actions that support the experiences she wishes to have

Many of these objectives I didn't understand. Centring myself? Shifting my emotional state? However, that didn't matter. I was so excited about the possibility of feeling better I signed the contract that day, December 18, 2014. Now I had a project, I had someone to guide me, and I had L3 holding me accountable. I had objectives, a structure, and even a timeline. As an achiever, this was my comfort zone. Before we got started on the program, though, Ean asked me to write a "future letter" to myself. In that letter, I was to thank myself for all that I had changed during the upcoming year of 2015. I wrote that letter in my office on a rainy January evening after my team had gone home.

Dear Claire,

I am writing this to sincerely congratulate you for all that you have achieved this year. You have transformed the way you think about yourself. I know it seemed like a bit of a pipe dream back then, but you have undergone a tremendous change and instilled habits that will enable you to lead a happy, energy-filled, loving life. Plus you have influenced those around you—you've spread your happiness, your experience, and wisdom so that you've not just changed yourself, you've started to have an impact on others as well. Here are some of the amazing things you have achieved this year.

Remember when you used to get so anxious about work that you wouldn't be able to sleep? You wouldn't be able to look past the next three months and you'd regularly entertain thoughts of just shutting the whole thing down? But now you think long term and you don't get obsessed about missing targets. You know your strategy, you know your brand through and through, you have the right people on the bus, and you're in the driver's seat. Your team fully believes in you and trusts you. You have become a strong leader.

Confession

Remember when you were unable to read about what your competitors were up to because it just made you feel like shit? Like you didn't measure up? Remember when you thought you were in the wrong industry and that you had nothing to add to the conversation? And now look at you—people know you and ask you to speak. You are building a strong reputation and people expect you to have an interesting point of view—they are excited to hear it! All that time you have spent reading, writing, and speaking has made a big difference both for Lux and for your personal brand.

Remember when you'd sit at L3 and you'd feel like you were so out of your league and that you had nothing to add to most of the conversations? You even told Yuri you were thinking about leaving the group because you felt like you had nothing to contribute and your fellow members were just putting up with you? But now you know you are having an impact—other members are learning from you and you know you have just as much right to be there as anybody else.

Remember when you used to get scared to learn about something you didn't know anything about because you were afraid to realize you'd been doing the "wrong" thing? Like investing and money management? You knew you should read those articles in the paper but you didn't really understand what they meant so you ignored them? And now you enjoy tackling something totally new. You may not get it right away, but you don't care. You don't have a fear of learning something new; in fact, you crave it!

Remember when you used to wake up and the first thing you thought was, "When can I sleep next?" Now you want to get up! You even smile sometimes when the alarm goes off! And you don't even use snooze anymore!

Remember when you were completely scattered about having kids? You didn't want them, you wanted your business and activities and hobbies more. You didn't want to change your relationship with Chris. You didn't want to be tied down. But you would second-guess yourself. You got so anxious about it you had to take sleeping pills. At night, you thought, "I'm not responsible for anyone! What is my purpose?" But now you're at peace because you know you won't have your own children, but you can have an impact in other ways. And now that you aren't your own worst enemy, you know you can make a difference and influence others. And you are exhilarated by that!

Remember when you'd be in a group of people you didn't know well? Like at a networking event or meeting friends of friends? And you'd get anxious and nervous and fantasize about the event just being done so you could get into bed with your book? And now you love meeting new people. You recognize that meeting new people means learning new things. And you are so much more confident now that you look forward to these events! And you don't even need wine to enjoy yourself!

Remember when you'd get so anxious and upset and literally hate yourself? And you used to feel yourself spiralling down into a pool of despair? And the only thought that made you feel a tiny bit better was "well, I could just die." And how that would sap all your energy and you couldn't even cry? And how you'd just feel life completely drain out of you such that the smallest task like watering the plants or folding the laundry would feel completely overwhelming?

Remember when "passive suicidal thoughts" were not irregular? And now, all you can do is give yourself such an

*enormous hug to make up for how sad you were. But you
have no regrets about any of those feelings. You needed them
to become the strong, confident, funny, successful, beautiful
person you are now.*

Congratulations to you. I love you.

Writing that letter is a vivid memory. The words flowed out
of me without hesitation. I also remember accidentally leaving
it on the printer that night and being mortified that one of my
employees may have read it. But the thing I remember most is
how difficult it was for me to write the last three words. I didn't
love myself—I didn't even like myself very much. In fact, when
I look at my journal round about the same time I wrote that letter, here is how I described myself: "I feel like a waste of skin."

As I read that letter back, I can see that I intuitively knew
what the antidote to achiever fever was. But back then I was
lost. I folded the letter up, put it in a pale pink envelope, and hid
it in my underwear drawer so that when I opened that drawer
daily I would be reminded of its existence. But I also kept it hidden because I was terrified that a year later I would read it and
nothing would have changed.

PART TWO
Fieldwork

Chapter 3

THE DIFFICULT PARTICIPANT

FIVE YEARS AGO, before this mesearch project began, someone asked me how well I thought I knew myself. On a scale of one to ten, they asked, with ten being I knew exactly who I was and one being I had no clue, where would I fall? I had recently taken Gallup's online StrengthFinders test, which spat out "achiever," "activator," and "maximizer," as my top strengths. Defining who I was through my strengths seemed obvious, and these words aligned with my self-definition, even if I didn't like myself very much. "Eight," I answered. A month into my work with Ean, I saw I would need to revise that number to about a three. And it was a focus group that made that realization possible.

Over the last twenty years, I have conducted more focus groups with as many different types of people than I can possibly count: gamblers, cardiologists, craft beer enthusiasts, car accident victims, NFL fans, fast food addicts, elderly seniors,

early technology adopters, accountants, even berry aficiona-
dos. And these are only a few of the people and groups I have
had in-depth conversations with. The focus group, long a staple
of market research, brings strangers into a room for a two-hour
conversation. As the moderator, it's my job to guide the discussion using a variety of questions and exercises to extract the
insights our clients are after.

Maybe you've seen a focus group on TV or perhaps you've
even participated in one, but they all tend to look about the
same. Eight to ten participants sit around a table in front of a
large one-way mirror, behind which sits the client, hidden from
view. These gatherings generally occur in the evening so that
participants can attend after work or school, or after taking care
of their families. When they arrive, their minds are still thick
with the day's activities and stresses, and my role is to get everyone comfortable with each other and build up the energy in the
room. I always begin by explaining what my role is and cover-
ing some ground rules, emphasizing that everyone has an equal
opportunity to share their opinions so that no one can dominate
the group.

In some focus groups, the conversation flows freely and my
job is easy. More often, I will have at least one or two "difficult" participants, and I must work a little harder to make sure
these people don't derail the session. As you might expect, a
cross-section of random human beings will always contain a few
interesting individuals. I remember one obviously stoned participant at a beer group who introduced himself as "Johnny 5,"
while holding his hand up and spreading his fingers to accentu-
ate the point. Surprisingly, the client elected to keep Johnny in
the group, which ended up being a good thing, because while
he was a little spacey, he was also one of the more creative

participants I've had. In small-town Alberta, I had a man who looked like a seventy-year-old Jesus, complete with a toga, who floated into the room and spent the next two hours staring at a wall. I've had a woman who breast pumped during the group, a guy who crouched behind his chair for much of the session, and a girl who repeatedly applied lipstick using the one-way mirror.

It doesn't matter where the group is—a specially designed facility, a food court, a bus, a hotel, a motel, an abandoned store in the middle of a mall—there are always participants that require a little more work than others: the teacher's pet, who usually sits right beside me at the table and needs to be the first to answer every question; the complainer who will find the downside of everyone else's ideas; the checked-out dude who keeps sneaking peaks at his phone under the table; the know-it-all; and the painfully shy. But the most difficult participant is the one who tends to sit directly across from me at the table, staring me down, arms crossed, slumped in his or her chair. This is the pissed-off, disgruntled participant who thinks this whole "focus group thing" is a load of bullshit. This one needs extra-special handling because they can take down the whole group with their negativity.

I was about to meet the most difficult participant I have ever had.

✦

FOR AS LONG as I can remember, I have been running from, or hiding from, a monster. The monster doesn't live in my closet or under my bed. It lives inside my head. Depending on the day, it will scream, snarl, or taunt me:

"You can't do this, you're going to fail!"
"You are such a fucking idiot!"
"You're so boring!"
"You're ugly. And you're fat!"
"Hah! You think you're a leader? Get real!"
"For God's sake, get your shit together and try harder!"

Ean got to meet the monster right away.

It was January, week one of our program. We'd decided that this week's personal training session would be in the climbing gym. There was a route I was trying to lead and it was at the top end of my abilities. I made it up the first few moves easily, struggled through the next few, and then got totally stymied once I got to the crux, the hardest move of the route. I had to put all my weight into my right bent leg, flag out my left, leap, and catch the hold above me. If I caught the hold, I had to quickly pull the rope up to clip the bolt before I lost my grip. Of the multiple times I had tried the route, I'd either miss the hold entirely, or not get a strong enough grip on it, and I would fall. And every time I fell, the monster would snarl: "You're a loser! You're weak! You're scared! You're not trying hard enough! You'll never finish this route!"

So when Ean asked me what I wanted to work on that first week of training, I pointed to the route and said, "That."

"OK," he responded. "Climb it. I'll watch you."

I got myself set up and started climbing. He'd call out little suggestions as I moved through it: hug the wall there, flag out on that hold, breathe, relax, but I could feel myself tense up as I approached the crux. He could see my hesitation and encouraged me from the ground, "Keep breathing, relax, go for it!" I set up for the move, wanting to impress him, and threw for the hold. This time I didn't even come close to catching it and I fell. "Fuck!" I yelled.

I was immediately embarrassed for swearing out loud, a rookie move in a climbing gym. That mistake alone was enough to get the monster in my head sneering and saying, "You'll never get it, you'll never get it!"

Ean lowered me down off the wall. My distress was obvious but he smiled at me. "All right," he said, "this seems like a pretty good place to start." As I write this now, I can see how it was the perfect place, the only place, really, to start. What I was about to learn over the next few weeks would fundamentally change me. Standing at the base of the route, Ean asked me several questions: "Were you focusing on your breathing?" No. "Did you visualize all the moves ahead of time?" No. "Did you climb that in a relaxed state?" Definitely not. "What happened?" he asked.

"I just feel like I'm never going to get it," I wailed. "I get so mad at myself."

He just looked at me, which I took as a cue to keep going.

"I get so worked up and I want it so badly. I have this voice in my head. It pushes me and pushes me and then it yells at me when I fall, and I just feel like shit and want to quit climbing and I hate everyone and everything."

"OK, great!" he exclaimed. "Here's something we can work on! Tell me more about this voice."

His question threw me. I'd never thought about it before. The voice was just there, as much a part of me as my internal organs. It had never occurred to me to question its existence because it had always been there, like a permanent house guest who moves in and trashes the place, forcing me to constantly clean up after it, and making me unsure if I was the host, the guest, or the garbage. The voice kept me tense and anxious and the only way to shut it up, it seemed, was to try and stay ahead of it. Up until the moment Ean asked me about it, I honestly believed that I was the only person with an inner voice this loud. "I feel like I'm the only one who has to deal with a voice this mean," I told him. "It makes me so hard on myself and I feel like I have it so much worse than anyone else!"

Ean laughed and said, "Claire, everybody has a voice in their head. Call it the inner critic, the gremlin, we all have it!"

I remember being shocked. Everyone walked around with a mean voice? I was speechless for a few seconds, and then spluttered, "OK fine, but mine is so much worse!"

Smiling, Ean said, "Trust me, it isn't. I know lots of people with a very similar sounding voice."

I felt floaty with relief. It wasn't just me.

Four years later, I asked the achievers in my survey about their inner critic. How strong was it on a scale of one to ten? The average score was an eight for women and a seven for men, with a third describing the strength of their inner critic at a nine or a ten. Interestingly, the follow-up question, "Are there a couple of negative thoughts or phrases that you tend to hear on repeat from your inner critic?" appeared more difficult to answer, with several electing not to answer at all. That didn't surprise me, as had I been asked this question when I first started working with Ean, I don't think I would have either. I would have felt too embarrassed and ashamed to admit what my voice said to me. But the honesty of the survey respondents who did write something was staggering. The predominant theme? *I am not enough.*

Achievers wrote about their inner voices telling them they were not good enough, smart enough, attractive enough, ambitious enough, hardworking enough, fit enough, or caring enough. One person wrote simply, "I've never been good enough and I will never be good enough." Another often-used word was "should"—with achievers reporting their inner critic telling them that they should be doing more, should be working harder, should understand, should be smarter, should try harder, should stop being an asshole. Then there were those who tied the two together: "If I tried harder, I'd be better." Or, "if I was better, I'd be happier."

Being called out as an imposter was another common thread in the survey responses: "You're a fraud, they'll figure you out soon." "You've tricked people into thinking you are capable and strong." "You should be an expert here but really you're not, you're just fooling everyone." "People will find out I don't know what I'm talking about."

The inner name caller was also fairly prevalent with "idiot" being the most common epithet: "What an idiot you are, how stupid can you be?" "What a fuck head!" "I did the wrong thing, I said the wrong thing, I didn't get enough done, I'm stupid, I'm lazy, I'm afraid, I'll never get it right, I'll never be satisfied."

There were also a few courageously honest respondents who pinpointed dark thoughts like: "Your life is meaningless." "There is something deeply wrong with you." "You should just die." My two favourite comments came from two seemingly self-aware achievers: "I always think others are smarter than me. I feel extraordinary joy when I see evidence they are not." And, "my voice replays the things I am most ashamed of... and then turns up the volume."

Whether we criticize our appearance, our intelligence, what we said, what we didn't say, what we should have said, the voice in our heads seems to tell us that we are not good enough the way we are. It tells us that we lack something, which, as I understand now, puts us in a state of need. Certainly this was my case.

Back then, I was convinced that if I could just accomplish this, or achieve that, the voice would finally shut up and I'd be at peace. Perhaps this is part of the reason almost seventy percent of the survey's achievers believe that they are going to be happier in the future than they are today.

✦

BACK IN THE climbing gym, it was time to get to know this difficult participant I had been dragging around with me all my life.

Ean asked who made me laugh. In 2015, that was an easy choice—Louis C.K. Ean said, "If Louis C.K. was listening to the voice in your head right now, what would he say?" Immediately, I could hear Louis's voice, dripping with sarcasm. He'd say something like: "Ooh, poor baby. What, are you upset that you're not a super hero, that you're a bad person because you can't climb up this plastic wall? Why the hell are you doing this in the first place?"

Imitating Louis's voice as best I could, I relayed this to Ean and couldn't help but laugh as I saw how ridiculous the voice now sounded. Ean encouraged me to climb the route again and, as I heard my inner voice, remember what C.K. would say. This time, I noticed myself smiling as I climbed, thinking about Louis C.K. shaking his head at me. I could tell I was more relaxed and the moves came easier and, for the first time, I sailed through the crux. Clipping into the anchors at the top, I whooped with celebration.

Back on the ground, I high-fived Ean and shook my head at him, grinning. "What happened?" I asked. "How did I do that?" Ean told me that I had taken the *power* out of the voice and that we would continue to work on this for the next couple of months. I left the gym that morning giddy with excitement. I had learned so much! I wasn't the only one with this nasty voice and I could beat it! Just sprinkle a little Louis C.K. on it and it went away. I was fixed!

Thirty minutes later, I was brushing my teeth and staring at my stomach in the mirror. "Ugh, so gross," said the voice. What? No! I panicked, trying to muster up Louis C.K. to drown it out, but I wasn't fast enough. The voice was now on a tear about my appearance, jumping from my stomach to my clothing to my hair to my face. I felt powerless to stop it, my confidence draining away with the water in the sink. Nothing had been fixed.

In our next session, I complained to Ean that the voice was still loud and clear. He asked me, "What does the voice look like?" Huh? What did it look like? Nothing, it was a voice. Ean encouraged me to shut my eyes and imagine what the voice might look like if it had a form. We ask our focus group participants to do exercises like this all the time: if this tech brand was a car, what would it be? But doing the same thing for the voice was strange. Feeling awkward and stupid, I shut my eyes and tried to visualize what it might look like.

Seeing that I was struggling, Ean then said exactly what we say to our market research participants: "Don't question it, don't analyze it. Just see the image and describe it." Immediately, an image came to mind—a gnarled, blackened, skinny, spiny tree stump, like a tree that had been in a forest fire. I described it to Ean. "Good," he said, "it has a form. Now, let's give it a name." This time, I didn't have to think. The name just fell out of my mouth: the Judge.

Ean told me that by naming something and making it into a describable object, we could take a good look at it. No longer hidden, we could shine a light on the voice and investigate it. Immediately I understood that this was where Ean's world and my world overlapped, and I realized I was now conducting my own, extremely personal focus group. I could visualize the table with me, the moderator, at one end, and at the other, the stump. It was even wearing a name tag: "Hello! My name is the Judge."

Now that I could see it, I wished I could do what I often wanted to do with difficult participants: eject them, just get them out of the room so my job was easier. Visualizing the Judge smirking at me from the end of the table, I said to Ean, "OK, great that it has a name and a form, but how do I get it out of my head? How can I burn this thing to the ground?" Ean told me it didn't work like that. If I wanted to take power away from it, he said, I needed to become intimately *aware* of it. He asked if I could remember when I first heard the Judge.

I closed my eyes and, within a few seconds, felt myself transported to the school playground as a seven-year-old. It was a sunny morning, maybe ten minutes before the first bell, and I was on my own, standing by the swings, watching all the various groups of kids cluster together, laughing and chatting excitedly. I described the scene to Ean.

"OK," he said, "hold yourself there. Hear the playground noises. Feel the sun. What is the Judge saying?" It was faint, like it was coming from oceans away, but I still could hear it: "You're all by yourself because you have no friends. No one wants to be your friend. You're not fun enough. You're boring."

As I replayed the words, repeating them to Ean, I was aghast at how awful they sounded. Ean then asked me how I felt when I heard those words. Tears sprang to my eyes as I remembered feeling lonely, anxious, and scared that all the other kids were making fun of me for being on my own. It also suddenly occurred to me that this was still a familiar feeling. Only a week earlier, looking for someone to talk to at a business event, I had experienced something similar.

Once Ean could see that I was reliving these childhood memories, he asked, "What would you say to that little girl if you could transport yourself back to that playground?" A feeling of tenderness rose up in my chest and I struggled to get the words out: "I'd wrap her up in my arms and hug her. I'd tell her everything was going to be OK, that she had absolutely nothing to worry about, that she was perfect the way she was. I would tell her I would always, always protect her."

I felt those words deeply. As I visualized that sad little girl, standing on her own by the swings, I was struck by how much love I felt for her. I was in tears now as I recognized how easy it was to love the "child me" and how impossible it seemed to love the "adult me." What had happened? What had I done to that kid? I cried as I saw that I hadn't loved and protected her throughout the years. This bully, the Judge, had made sure of it. Tears streaming down my face, I said to Ean, "I can't believe I've been listening to this voice for decades. I wouldn't say what I say to myself to my worst enemy! I didn't protect that little girl and I haven't protected her since!" Ean looked at me. "And yet look at what you've built," he said, "a successful business, good friends, a great relationship. You don't think you've protected yourself?"

I saw what he was getting at. The phenomenon of the Judge was more complex. Yes, the voice had made me miserable, but it had also propelled me to succeed in life. It may have beaten me up, but it made me strong. My work ethic was fostered to stave off the Judge's guilty verdict, and my competitive spirit was developed to buy stays of conviction. I had to admit the Judge had been useful and I said this to Ean.

He encouraged me to thank the Judge for all that it done for me over the years—to look at this gnarled tree stump and voice my appreciation for the motivation and drive it had given me. Feeling very strange, I hesitatingly thanked it out loud, but now I was confused. Yes, I wanted to get rid of it but also saw that I seemed to need it. If I didn't have the Judge anymore, would my ambition die? Would I lose my competitive spirit? Ean told me I had a choice. I could give it power by listening to it. Or I could ignore it because like any bully, the more I ignored it, the less powerful it would become. By ignoring it, he said, I might start to hear some other voices, voices who had maybe been there all along but who had been drowned out by the Judge. Now I understood that if I wanted to hear from these other participants around my focus group table, I had to stop the Judge from dominating the conversation.

For the next few weeks, I was very aware of the Judge. Like when you get a new car and suddenly you see that same car everywhere. The Judge was there. All. The. Time. Nattering away at me from the moment I woke up—"If you don't get up and work out, you'll get fat!"—and at the swimming pool—"Swim faster, you were so much stronger yesterday!" It sprang up when I was heading to the car—"You're going to be late, get your shit together!"—and at work—"He's looking at you like you have no idea what you're talking about"—and on and on. Constant jabbering.

The Judge seemed to have moved from the back of my head to right between my eyes. Sometimes, when I caught it saying something particularly mean, I tried to visualize it as that gnarled tree stump. When this happened, I had a choice to tune in or tune out. But I'd been tuned into the Judge on autopilot for so long, changing the station seemed impossible. Sometimes,

I would find myself in a horrible mood and realize hours later that the Judge had been in session the whole time. For example, I would do a three-hour drive down to Seattle in a funk, feeling beaten up when I finally arrived. It was only when I parked the car that I realized the Judge had been at work. Or, we'd lose a project at work, and I'd go hiking at the end of the day and at the top of the mountain realize I couldn't remember any of the climb because the Judge had been my hiking partner.

When I mentioned this to Ean, he reassured me that by becoming aware of these times when the Judge was dominating the conversation, I was making good progress. Only a few weeks earlier, it had never occurred to me to question the existence of this inner critic and now I could recognize, though not always immediately, when the Judge was talking to me. Most importantly, I was starting to understand that the Judge wasn't me, but a component of me.

Back when we had first met to discuss my objectives, Ean had told me that change can only come from awareness. Now I understood better what he meant. Only when we become aware of something can we change it. This, he had said, was internal work. Just like we spend time exercising our physical selves, or our "outside" selves, we also need to exercise our "internal" selves. I may have been physically strong, but internally, I was blindly allowing myself to get carried along by the Judge. This internal work, Ean told me, required real strength.

Like an addict trying to kick their habit, I was encouraged to pay attention to when the Judge was triggered. I had to catch it in action. Only when I was aware of it talking could I change the conversation, so Ean taught me an exercise to help me do this. At the end of each day, I had to write down three instances where the Judge came up. I would then score my reaction to each instance, on a scale of one to four. I would give myself a "1" if I had let the Judge yack away at me and didn't notice until hours later. My after-work hike or trip to Seattle would be examples of this. A "2" would be for when I became aware of the Judge harping away in real time, but I couldn't stop it or tune in to something different. If I became aware of the Judge and made a conscious decision to change the station, usually by focusing on something else, like striking up a conversation with someone, listening to music, or immersing myself in a task to the point that I could no longer hear the Judge, I could give myself a "3." A "4" happened when the Judge didn't make an appearance when it normally would otherwise. For example, if I was flailing through an easy climbing route and the Judge didn't show up at all.

Paying careful attention to when the Judge made an appearance was my first exercise in self-awareness. Each evening, for the next few weeks, I would think back over the day and jot down a few instances of the Judge showing up. Though my journal was filled with mostly ones and the occasional two, I could see how paying attention to something was the foundation for change. This exercise was forcing me not just to notice, but also to amplify these instances of my inner critic by grading them. It was a perfect exercise for an achiever; I wanted to turn those ones into fours.

I didn't do this writing exercise every night. Sometimes I didn't want to think back through the day because it had been so awful and I knew I would get all ones, and sometimes I just wanted to read my book and not do the work to write anything down. But as the weeks went by, I started to see a few more twos and even the occasional three. Sometimes, as I made my notes in my journal, the Judge would start up and say, "You can't get past a two, you'll never get to four, why are you bothering?" I would catch these moments and, suddenly, I had a three on my hands when I realized I wasn't giving in to it and instead continuing with the exercise.

While doing this exercise, I soon realized that there were hundreds, maybe thousands, of moments each day where the Judge would flare up. Some I caught, most I didn't. Sometimes, I would be floating merrily along like a raft in a river when suddenly the Judge would appear out of nowhere, and I would find myself feeling like I was thrashing around in Class Four rapids. I'd clue in because my body would go tense and my breathing would get shallow. I noticed that if I told the Judge to fuck off, it got worse. In fact, I noticed that the more I wanted it to go away, the louder it seemed to get. I realized this was the same thing that happened sometimes when I was trying to sleep. The harder I tried, the more elusive it became. What do I do, I asked Ean, when I am aware of the Judge but I can't seem to stop listening to it? The more I want it to shut up, the louder it gets.

Ean suggested that rather than trying to shout over the voice or demand that it go away, I could try "acting as if" it hadn't said anything. The power, he explained, came through the action I took, regardless of what the Judge told me to do. A few days later something happened that showed me exactly how that could work. A close friend texted to tell me they had just bought a house. As I was reading the text, the Judge was sneering and saying that I was "just a loser renter" and I felt pulled to ignore my friend's message.

It was alarming how difficult the idea of simply texting my congratulations felt. On the one hand, I wanted to be the sort of person who naturally celebrated my friends' successes. On the other hand, I could see how consumed with jealousy I was. Recognizing this, I elected to push myself and call the friend. By the end of the conversation, I felt sincerely happy for her. As I wrote about the experience later in my journal, a familiar phrase came to mind, "I've got to get out of my own way." Was that what I had done?

✦

A COUPLE OF months later, I took a cab home with an employee. We had just finished presenting the results of a survey to a client. She had done a great job presenting, I told her, but she didn't agree. She said, "I just don't feel like I have the confidence to be a good presenter." I told her she was wrong, that I had just seen her present well. "You're a great presenter," I told her. "You thinking you're not is all in your head."

I smiled inwardly as I said it, realizing she was struggling with her own voice, and I encouraged her to tell me how she felt. She explained that she was constantly fighting herself, trying hard to boost herself up but falling victim to feeling like she just wasn't good enough. We were nearing the end of our cab ride, and I told her I was dealing with something similar. I told her that I had a voice in my head that told me terrible things about myself. She stared at me, shocked, and said, "But you're always so confident!" I was a little shocked as well, watching myself say this out loud to an employee, but I shrugged and said, "I hide it well." The next day, she asked if I had heard of a podcast called *The One You Feed*. I shook my head, I hadn't. I downloaded an episode the next day and played it in my car. After a burst of music, the host, Eric Zimmer, came on to say:

Welcome to The One You Feed. *Throughout time, great thinkers have recognized the importance of the thoughts we have. Quotes like "garbage in, garbage out" or "you are what you think" ring true and yet, for many of us, our thoughts don't strengthen or empower us. We tend towards negativity, self-pity, jealousy, or fear. We see what we don't have instead of what we do. We think things that hold us back and dampen our spirit.*

This sounded familiar. Zimmer then explained that he started every episode with the same parable:

A grandfather is talking to his grandson. The grandfather says, "In life, there are two wolves inside of us that are always at battle. One is a good wolf which represents things like kindness and bravery and love, and the other is a bad wolf which represents things like greed, hatred, and fear." The grandson stops and thinks about it for a second and looks up at his grandfather and says, "Grandfather, which one wins?" And the grandfather replies, "The one you feed."

Tears sprung to my eyes, I saw the connection right away. The Judge was my bad wolf, but was I feeding it, or was it feeding me? By listening to the Judge, I was feeding it negative thoughts, which it would then play back to me. *The One You Feed* became another source of access to people—philosophers, psychologists, neuroscientists, and artists—who were willing to talk about the inner voice. As I listened to episode after episode, one question became clear: why do we have this voice in the first place if it causes us so much grief? I was fortunate enough to have a colleague, a McGill and Harvard-trained medical doctor named Dr. Lara Patriquin, to help guide me through the literature of neuroscience and cognitive psychology to help me understand what might be happening.

Dr. Patriquin is a radiologist and a speaker and coach on mental well-being. Recently she had the opportunity to interview Dr. Michael Gazzaniga, founder of the Center for Cognitive Neuroscience at University of California, Davis, about this inner voice. Through his experiments with split-brain patients, it was Gazzaniga who gave the "voice in our heads" a name: the left-brain interpreter.[5]

In an effort to isolate seizures in epileptic patients to one side of the brain, surgeons in the 1940s used a procedure to cut through the corpus callosum, the bridge that joins the two sides of the brain together. These operations produced several split-brain patients who were subsequently studied by Gazzaniga. He wanted to learn how the two sides of the brain operated, and his experiments showed that not only do the left and right brain process information very differently, they also operate quite separately from each other.[6]

In one experiment, he asked the isolated right brain of a split-brain patient to stand up and walk to the door. The person did so. The left brain was cognizant that the person had gotten up but wouldn't have known why. When Gazzaniga asked the left brain why the person had stood up, he was surprised by the response. Rather than simply say they didn't know, the person created a reason for getting up: "I wanted to get a can of pop." The left brain had made up a story.[7]

The left brain, or more accurately, a component of the brain in the frontal lobe of the left side, coined the "left-brain interpreter," is the part of our brain that narrates our life for us— it is our constant internal monologue. Shut your eyes for ten seconds and try not to hear the narrator. It's impossible—the voice is always there. To keep our lives manageable, the left-brain interpreter looks for an internally consistent, coherent narrative. The trouble comes when the left-brain interpreter makes assumptions. In order to explain what is happening as it happens, it will look for the easiest explanation as speed is of the essence. But the easiest explanation is not always a factual one.

Dr. Patriquin explained to me that the left-brain interpreter evolved to keep our species alive. It takes in sights and sounds and smells, scrolling through memories and thoughts for connections, and quickly creates a story, which drives our narrative and our decision-making. It is impulsive and superficial and will often jump to the worst-case scenario.

I saw my left-brain interpreter in action while I was on a weekend getaway with Chris. Upon leaving the office I told my team to contact me only in the case of emergency. On day two of my trip, I entered my hotel room to see a red light blinking on the cordless desk phone. I was immediately seized with panic assuming the light meant something was wrong—a cash flow issue or a pissed-off client. Or maybe something had happened to my family—someone was sick or someone had died. These were the thoughts coursing through my brain in the length of time it took me to cross the room. Leaning in to check the phone, I saw a word beside the red light: charging. Nothing more. My left-brain interpreter had seized on the red light keeping me in a state of stress until I was able to factually ascertain that there was nothing to be concerned about.

Dr. Patriquin explained to me that the left-brain interpreter is language-based. It needs language to generate a narrative and contrives stories based on the language we use internally. For example, if we say "I always fail at this," or "I never seem to get that right," when we do indeed fail at that thing, or don't get that thing right, our theory is validated and the assumption is made credible. The left-brain interpreter doesn't look for instances that contradict those assumptions, when thing *did* go right or when we *didn't* fail at something, because that is not its function. It doesn't require context or debate, just a quick explanation. So, when we have reoccurring negative thoughts about ourselves, the interpreter uses that internal language as the easy way to explain whatever is occurring. If we have the thought, I'm so depressed, the interpreter assumes we are depressed and processes information so that it is aligned with that thought. It becomes a self-fulfilling prophecy. As Dr. Patriquin writes, "The problem is that, like wildfires or seizures, we have allowed the left-brain interpreter to go into hyperdrive and be the dominant brain function that drives our existence. We believe its every word.... The interpreter has gone from being a trusted servant to an imperious master."[8]

With the left-brain interpreter as a guide to the world, you can understand why you might be your harshest critic or worst enemy. Dr. Patriquin emphasized we will not know how to most effectively question the left-brain interpreter until we understand how the brain works in its entirety (and bear in mind that the brain is unbelievably complex), and that the interpreter theory will no doubt become much more nuanced as we learn more. What is most important to remember is that our internal narrative is not necessarily the truth and that the left-brain interpreter may be what is keeping us in an unnecessarily negative space.

What Dr. Patriquin told me next was something I had already experienced, but I hadn't understood why. When I attempted to change the channel on the Judge and quiet its voice, this was more easily done if I immersed myself in a different activity. Dr. Patriquin told me that what I had done, albeit unknowingly, was to deliberately cultivate an experience that turned up the volume in my right brain where creativity and intuition are located.

She asked if I'd ever seen or heard something so beautiful I was rendered speechless. I could easily recall being transported by music, remembering concerts where I had been so emotionally overwhelmed by a song that I felt outside of myself—in that moment, there was an absence of the inner voice. Dr. Patriquin then asked if I could remember being in the flow of something, a sport, a hobby, or even work, where time seemed to stop. Again, I could recall several occasions where I had been so involved in what I was doing, I had completely lost track of time and, seemingly, myself. Being in the "zone" was an effective way of dialling down that inner voice so that life could be conducted intuitively.

But how, I asked Dr. Patriquin, can we possibly string together enough of these types of experiences to create a more enjoyable life for ourselves? She told me that the other way we can turn down the volume of our left-brain interpreter is to simply remember that it makes assumptions, and so we cannot trust the stories we tell ourselves. It may be our brain, but we cannot believe it is telling us the truth. Becoming aware of the Judge and recognizing it was making up untruths was shifting my foundations of understanding. I recalled my colleague asking me how well I knew myself. The honest answer was not at all, but I simply didn't know enough to know that.

I thought back to my personal focus group and saw the gnarled tree stump in its chair. Still formidable, but maybe slightly less difficult. I suddenly became aware of the vacant chairs around the table and remembered Ean saying that once the Judge became less dominant, I may start to hear some other voices. Who else was in this focus group with me? Ean turned the question back to me: who did I want to put in those chairs? Here is what I wrote in my journal that night:

- *A thinker*—someone who loves reading, writing, and contemplating
- *A wanderer*—someone who follows their curiosity without needing a destination
- *A comedian*—someone who brings delight and laughter to themselves and others
- *A coach*—someone who passionately supports others in their endeavours
- *A creator*—someone who gives themselves the freedom to engage with the depths of their creative spirit

Wow—who were these people? As I described them to Ean the next day, I visualized them sitting around the table. They all took up the same amount of space as the Judge. Just like any other focus group I had conducted, I saw there was no hierarchy; each had their right to their opinion. But there was something tugging at me—an empty chair, a void that I couldn't quite visualize but felt important, even necessary. Suddenly an image came to me—the sun. Ultimately, this is who I wanted to be. This is the voice I wanted to listen to—a sun shining brightly, warming, illuminating. I wanted to feel energized, exuberant, and exhilarated. I wanted to shine for myself and others around me. I explained this to Ean and he encouraged me to try and visualize my sun sitting in its own chair. A few seconds later, I could see it very faintly at the far end of the room. It was covered in clouds, but, if I squinted, it was there.

How, I asked Ean, do I get to know all these new participants? What should I do next? He said, "Just like you practice all the things you do, now you need to practice who you want to be."

If I wanted to find my sun, I had to get rid of the fog.

Chapter 4

SLAVE TO THE "FACTS"

My co-worker Hanson sometimes picks me up on the way to work. We have our routine down to the second. When he arrives, I open the back door, toss my bag in, and say hello to his dog, a Shiba Inu named Kiba. Then I open the front door, sit down in the passenger seat, and say something like, "Hey dude, how's it going, thanks for picking me up." Hanson turns down the radio and then pulls back into the street. Before he is at the end of the block, he does something that drives me crazy. He lowers both of our windows down a few inches. He does it every time, and every time this is what goes through my head: oh my God, my breath must smell! As we chat about what our days look like, I'm thinking, What did I eat last night? Did I eat garlic? Do I have a problem? I've got to floss more. I need to book a trip to the dentist. Why don't I see the dentist more often? Are my gums receding? Keeping up with the conversation, as these unsavoury thoughts are unspooling through my brain, drains whatever energy I had left over from my early morning workout. When we get into work, my desk seems heavy with challenges.

This happened for an embarrassing number of years. But one day, after practicing Ean's "notice the Judge" exercise for a few weeks, I caught my inner voice as Hanson lowered the window. I watched it make me feel worried and anxious. If I wanted to change the script, I knew I had to act. It took a couple more trips to work up the courage and then, one morning: "Hey dude! Hi Kiba!" I said as I opened the back door to dump my bag. I got in the front seat and Hanson lowered the windows. Nervously, I said, "Hey, can I ask you a question?"

"Sure, what's up?" Hanson asked.

"Every time I get into your car, you lower the windows. Why do you do that?" I could feel my back tightening, preparing for the worst.

"Because I'm worried my car stinks of dog and I don't want you to smell it," he said.

I released my breath. I hadn't realized I'd been holding it.

"Seriously?" I asked. "That's why you put down the windows? All this time I thought it was my breath!"

Hanson laughed and said, "No! I was always thinking you thought my car stunk!"

We assured each other that there was no bad breath and no dog smell. When I walked into the office that morning, my desk seemed full of promise.

Later when I recounted the story for Ean, I explained that I had felt a surge of almost giddy confidence when I realized the truth. Ean told me I had done two important things: first, I had paid attention to my thoughts in real time and second, rather than accepting them on autopilot, I had questioned them. Continuing to practice this, he said, would challenge and change my thinking. I believed him. The car ride example seemed so innocuous but it opened my eyes to how easily I manufacture beliefs. Every occurrence of the lowered window offered further proof to support my belief that Hanson thought my breath smelled. I had turned a belief into a "fact." How many other "facts" had I created?

The maddening thing about the takeaway from this story is that I already know people make stuff up. My career is based on understanding people's perceptions, their beliefs, and the stories they tell themselves. I understand that behind those perceptions are all sorts of irrational theories, filters, biases, emotions, and false memories. As I tell my clients, market research does not provide truth but rather direction and guidance. We study people, which means we are not dealing with facts. Yes, a huge sample size for a survey can provide a level of "certainty" but we are still at the mercy of self-reported behaviour. At the beginning of every focus group, I emphasize to my participants that I am looking for their perceptions and opinions and that I am not interested in facts. I tell them there is no such thing as a right or wrong answer.

I know that our research participants make up stories. Sometimes, it's because they want to impress, by downplaying the number of alcoholic beverages consumed in a week, for example, or by telling me they always recycle when a quick glance in their garbage proves otherwise. Usually, it's an innocent mistake like getting products mixed up, misremembering what they last paid for groceries, or saying they are aware of a brand we've made up. My job is to dig below the surface because I can't take all of what they say at face value. Why had I never thought to apply this to myself? I didn't realize it then, but self-discovery is like a tap you can't turn off. I was about to get hit with a deluge.

I go to a lot of market research conferences at which I spend two or three days listening to dozens of speakers on what's new in the industry. When I sat down to hear a talk in San Diego about a new discipline called behavioural economics, I had no idea how powerful it would prove to be in both my personal and professional life. It was an image of an iceberg that first caught my attention. The speaker was using it as an analogy to explain how we make decisions. She told us that our conscious brain, the part of the brain we have access to, was the tip sticking out of the water. Much more interesting, however, is the larger bulk of the iceberg hidden underwater. This, the speaker said, is our subconscious and unconscious mind, the part of our brain that we don't have access to, but is responsible for more than ninety percent of our cognitive activity.[9]

As I listened to the presentation, I remembered Fan saying that the only way to change something was to become conscious of it. I used to be unconscious of the Judge until I brought it up from the depths by talking about it. When I realized that my personal and professional interests were intertwining, my attention intensified. The speaker explained that less than ten percent of our decisions are based on rational thinking. For these decisions, we use the slow and methodical problem-solving part of our brain. The large majority of our decisions are made quickly, instinctively and, as behavioural economists have proved, often irrationally. These are the decisions that remain hidden from us. We can't explain them because we are not conscious of them. I wondered, listening to the speaker, how we could ever hope to understand our research participants if they are unaware of their own decisions?

Back home, I immediately dove into books and articles by behavioural economists like Dan Ariely, Daniel Kahneman, and Richard Thaler. To understand how this discipline works, we need to return to high school economics when we learned about Adam Smith, one of the forefathers of the Age of Reason. Thinkers like Smith posited that human beings are reasonable creatures who make rational decisions that further their own self-interest. "It is not from the benevolence of the butcher, the brewer, or the baker that we expect our dinner", he wrote, "but from their regard to their own interest." This assumption is famous in economics.[10]

But towards the end of the twentieth century, psychologists began to question this assumption.[11] Their experiments proved that humans often act irrationally and make decisions that do not have our best interests in mind. (It is not in my best interest to eat chips, but I do. It is not in my best interest to ignore a co-worker, but I do.) In fact, these psychologists found that not only are most of our decisions not rational, many are not helpful. We use mental shortcuts to make quick decisions and these shortcuts are buried deep in our subconscious. We make decisions based on social norms, what our parents did, what we are familiar with, what makes us comfortable, what we did last time, habits, what we think will make us look good, and the list goes on. The problem is, behavioural economists point out, these shortcuts lead to biased, non-rational decision-making. By understanding these cognitive biases, as they call them, we can develop a more nuanced understanding of human behaviour.[12] Until then we will remain "strangers to ourselves."

That phrase, also the title of a book by the French philosopher Julia Kristeva, captivated me. I was doing this mesearch project because I wanted to, as Socrates advised, "Know Thy-self." So I decided to use myself as a guinea pig to explore just a few of these dozens of cognitive biases.

CONFIRMATION BIAS is our tendency to pay much stronger attention to information that confirms our beliefs and hypotheses than to information that doesn't. If I have a suspicion that we have lost a project to another firm, I will inflate the meaning of information that supports that hypothesis. For example, if the potential client does not return my call, I am more likely to see this as evidence they are talking to the competition as opposed to the possibility that they might be stuck in a meeting. When I look back at the proposal, I see its weaknesses, not its strengths. I even spend the evening feeling disappointed only to find out the next day that we have won the project. I see confirmation bias at play when I do reference checks on a new employee I really like and listen more intently to the positive comments than to the negative. More fright ening is when I am believing I am not good enough and see evidence everywhere to support my belief. Yep. I defi-nitely suffer from confirmation bias.

The **LOSS AVERSION BIAS** refers to our tendency to strongly prefer avoiding losses than to acquiring gains. That is, we would much rather not lose something than we would rather gain something. Studies show that losses are perceived to be twice as powerful as gains. Rationally, this doesn't make any sense. We should be able to draw up a list of pros and cons and weigh them equally in our minds. But they don't feel equal. Potential losses weigh much heavier on us than potential gains. This helps explain why some people stay in relationships longer than they should. Eight years into my relationship with my ex-husband, I knew our situation was not good for either of us. However, the spectre of losing my "married status," disappointing our families, splitting up the house and the dog, and walking away from the "investment" of several years together seemed considerably more powerful than what I might gain: time on my own, discovering new people and activities, meeting someone better suited to me. Biased thinking meant I stayed in the relationship longer than I should have. The loss aversion bias happens at work as well. My decision-making around opening a second office put far more weight on the cost to get it started than it did on the amount of business a new market would bring. I now keep this natural bias in mind when I'm in decision-making mode.

POWER OF THE DEFAULT is another cognitive bias that causes us to default to a behaviour because it is what we're used to—not because it is right or useful. The power of the default bias is what makes change so difficult. Because the familiar is easy and change is scary, we often repeat what we've done in the past, regardless of whether it makes sense for us in the present. I spent years feeling crappy and anxious before I made the decision to start my mesearch project and work with Ean. Had I not defaulted back to blindly accepting my life as it was, I could have started this self-discovery process much earlier. Defaulting to the familiar dominance of the Judge is another powerful example of this bias.

The NEGATIVITY BIAS is perhaps one of the most interest-ing of these cognitive biases. We exhibit the negativ-ity bias when we place more emphasis and weight on negative thoughts and experiences rather than on pos-itive thoughts or experiences. This bias is a core issue of discussion in *The One You Feed* podcast; why do we feed our "bad wolves" more easily than our good ones? Behavioural psychologists note that a compliment may feel good for a few minutes but a perceived insult will stay with us for much longer. In fact, studies show that negative emotions and thoughts are five times more pow-erful than positive ones, especially since we tend to rumi-nate on the negative thoughts. Amazingly, to overcome one negative thought, we need to hear or experience at least five positive things.[13] The negativity bias helped to explain my funks. Once I was in a negative headspace, I would also use the confirmation bias to find further proof for feeling bad, which dragged me deeper into despair.

These are four of the more common biases researchers are aware of. By exploring them, I could easily see how irrational my thinking was. Around this time, I saw an optical illusion on my Twitter feed. It was a photo of what looked like a pebble lodged in a brick wall. I stared, squinted, blinked, and held my phone at different angles trying to see the secret. After several minutes, I still hadn't grasped the mystery of this illusion. When I finally clicked on the link to reveal the answer, I gasped out loud. The pebble wasn't a pebble but the ash end of a cigar poking out of the brick wall, obscured by a curious photo perspective and camou-flaged by similar colours. How could I not have seen it? But, more importantly, now that I had seen it, I couldn't unsee it.

This is how I felt two months into my mesearch project as I discovered the Judge, the left-brain interpreter, and these cognitive biases. I had scrolled through decades of my life without stopping to examine how I felt about myself. Now that I had decided to pay closer attention, insights were being revealed to me that I couldn't unsee. It was exhilarating. But I also felt overwhelmed. None of these new processes were something I could do by rote—they required attention. I had to remember to listen for the Judge, make notes in my journal, be cognizant of Ean's number system, do the "act as if" exercise, and now I also had to think about which of the myriad cognitive biases might be at work in my decision-making. Yes, my goal was to keep uncovering useful insights about myself, but it required so much work! All the articles on behavioural economics that I hadn't yet read—more work! And, when I heard the Judge pipe up, my first thought was not pleasure that I'd caught it, but annoyance thinking how many times I'd probably missed it that day already—more work! Goddamnit! I wanted to be good at this! I had to laugh. I was experiencing achiever fever trying to wake up from achiever fever. Surely there had to be an easier way to identify and question this biased, irrational thinking of mine? Now that I was looking, of course, there was.

I was at Ean's house waiting for him to finish up with another client. I was bored and trying not to check my phone so I could keep my mind clear before our session, but I needed something to do so I picked up a book from his coffee table. The title, *Loving What Is*, seemed soft and bland to me. The front cover was a photo of a kind-looking, middle-aged woman, the author, I assumed, who also had an unusual name, Byron Katie. I surmised the book was some sort of self-help or personal affirmation book. As I flipped through the introduction I froze when

I read this, "Whenever we experience a stressful feeling—anything from mild discomfort to intense sorrow, rage, or despair—we can be certain that there is a specific thought causing our reaction, whether we are conscious of it or not. The way to end our stress is to investigate the thinking that lies behind it."[14] I sensed a connection with what I'd been learning about in behavioural economics. But, as I read a little further this was the kicker, "When we believe our thoughts instead of what is really true for us, we experience the kinds of emotional distress we call suffering."[15]

The Judge had been the mass producer of my thoughts for a long time. I had believed them and had experienced a good amount of emotional distress as a result. Even with her strange name and the easy-going title, I decided Byron Katie had something interesting to say. I asked Ean if I could borrow the book and started reading it the next day. Just like her name, Byron Katie was one-of-a-kind. A mother of three kids, she had spent over a decade consumed by anxiety and depression. Eventually, she got so down that she checked herself into a halfway house, convinced that she would rather be dead. Then, one morning, she woke up and realized there was nothing actually wrong with her. She had been so wrapped up in her own negative thoughts that she couldn't see what was real. Her sudden awareness that she had been a prisoner of her thoughts was a profound, shocking wake-up.

This experience of waking up was so powerful; she felt she had no choice but to share it with others. She went on to develop a system of self-inquiry she called "The Work" that others could use, first, to recognize when they were imprisoning themselves with their own stressful thoughts and, second, to learn how to break out of their self-imposed jails. Byron

Katie is very open about how The Work functions and the information is available to anyone free of charge on her website. What follows is simply my experience with it (written with the benefit of several months intense practice, as well as attending the nine-day School for The Work in 2017). I have come to rely on The Work as a tool that teaches me how to think rationally and clearly. It is also the best weapon I have found to deal with the Judge.

A few years ago, I was convinced that my financial advisor was scamming me. I was certain that the performance of my portfolio was worse than everyone else's. I would wrestle with this knot of worry as I tried to fall asleep, getting myself more worked up. Using the process of The Work, I was able to work through my fear and anxiety around the situation and deconstruct the illusions I had cast upon it.

The first step of The Work consists of first identifying a painful thought. Identifying a painful thought is easy because often we feel it. The stress, fear, doubt, sadness, or frustration we feel is an indication that we are attached to, or believing, that thought. Once the thought that is causing us pain is identified, Byron Katie encourages people to frame the thought in the form of a statement of judgment and identify the cause as another person, as this is our natural tendency anyway in painful situations: it's another person's fault that I feel this way. I blamed the performance of my financial portfolio on my advisor. Surely, he was ripping me off! So, I wrote down my belief in the form of a judgment: my financial advisor is ripping me off.

The next step of The Work was to answer four easy but powerful questions about the judgment:

1. Is it true?
2. Can you absolutely know it's true?
3. How do you react, what happens when you believe that thought?
4. Who would you be without the thought?

My answer to question one, is it true that my financial advisor is ripping me off, was an immediate "Yes!"

Time for question two. Can you absolutely know that it's true? My first instinct was to say yes, of course, it's true. But, after thinking about it carefully, I had to acknowledge that I had to say no. The question asks if I could *absolutely* know. In a court of law, I could not testify that I was 100 percent sure that I was being ripped off, as I had no factual evidence to back up that assertion.

Time for question three. How do you react, what happens when you believe that thought? How do I react when I think my advisor is ripping me off? All I needed to do was remember the roll call of nightmarish thoughts rushing through my head as I was trying to sleep. I feel paranoid, scared that I have made a bad decision, that I'm being duped, that my father would be disgusted with me for being taken in by this guy, like I'd learned nothing from my dad, which makes me feel sad and pitiful. I feel like a kid who hasn't grown up. I feel stupid and uneducated. I feel full of self-doubt and anger for not better understanding my finances. The whole topic makes me feel so uncomfortable I'd rather just ignore it than learn more about it, which makes me feel lazy and weak. That's a lot of angst. No wonder I couldn't sleep when I thought about my financial advisor.

Time for question four. Who would you be without that thought? This question can stop you in your tracks if you find it difficult to imagine not having a specific thought once you've attached yourself to it. Not surprisingly, it took me a few minutes to answer. Without the thought that my financial advisor is ripping me off, I would be able to approach the subject rationally. I'd be present, focused, and attentive. I would be more understanding and patient with myself, recognizing that finances are not a comfortable subject for me. I would slow down and take my time when I talked to my financial advisor. I would enjoy learning about my finances. If I did see or hear something that didn't seem right, I would ask for more detailed explanations without any fear. I'd be grateful for the money I do have and excited about planning for the future. I would also recognize that I don't know what my colleagues' returns are, and maybe I would open a conversation with them so we could all learn more.

By imagining who I could be without the story I had told myself, I knew I had the potential to be that person I described in question four. But to become that person I needed to stop believing this thought, which, as question two showed me, I could not know absolutely was true anyway. Unfortunately, no strange magic was going to make me stop believing a thought so deeply ingrained. I appeared to be trapped.

Byron Katie understands how we can get imprisoned by our thoughts, and so she came up with what she calls the "turnarounds" to address this. In this process, you take the original statement and turn it around to its opposite, to the self, and to the other. For each turnaround, you look for at least three examples that are as true, if not truer, than the original statement.

Original Statement: *My financial advisor is ripping me off.*
Turnaround 1 (to the opposite): My financial advisor is *not* ripping me off.

1. I don't *know* that he is, I just *think* he is. My thoughts have frequently been incorrect before, so there is a good chance they are incorrect now.
2. My advisor has several other clients that sing his praises. I've met them at events his firm hosts. These longstanding clients have no concerns about him ripping them off, so it does not make any sense that he would single me out as someone to rip off.
3. I am doing my previous due diligence a disservice. Before I chose this advisor to work with, I researched others and found that their fees were either similar or sometimes even more expensive.

This turnaround statement had me start doubting my original belief.

Turnaround 2 (to the other): *I* am ripping my financial advisor off.

1. He's spent hours trying to educate me about my finances, but I've been so fearful of looking stupid, I haven't given him my full attention. I am wasting his time and, in effect, I am ripping him off.
2. He is in this relationship with me for the long haul but I am not letting him prove it
3. I'm not giving him any benefit of the doubt and I've labelled him "guilty" with no proof.

Now I was starting to realize how my lack of education and fear had been a barrier. They were preventing my financial advisor from being able to do his job properly. Suddenly, I could see that perhaps I was the problem, not him.

Turnaround 3 (to the self): *I'm* ripping *myself* off.

1. I chose this firm after a good amount of research, asking my peers and listening to other financial advisors pitch me for my business. I am not giving myself the credit for making a well-researched decision to go with him in the first place.
2. I am robbing myself of an opportunity to develop a stronger relationship with my advisor, as well as an opportunity to better understand my finances.
3. By second-guessing myself I spend hours fretting and robbing myself of sleep!

Once I worked through these three turnarounds, a shift started to happen in my thinking. It was no longer black and white but full of grey areas. My lack of focus and education was perhaps the culprit here, not my advisor. The turnarounds shed light on the situation so that I could see it from several different angles, but they also provided a prescription for action: I could tell my advisor how I feel. Admit that I don't understand how my fees work. Ask him to show me in detail, ask him to compare my returns to other firms. Pay close attention to what he is saying and then decide to either look for someone else or move forward and build a strong relationship with him.

Byron Katie's system works because it is experiential. Working through the questions forces us to deconstruct our beliefs. No one is telling us what to do. We are creating our own prescription for future behaviour based on our own rational thinking. The Work slows us down so that we can see and cut through our biases. Katie believes there is no belief that cannot be diffused by The Work. Four years after my mesearch project began, I have yet to find one.

Today I have a great relationship with my financial advisor because I identified the stressful thought, questioned it, and recognized that my original belief about him simply wasn't true. I followed the prescription from the turnarounds, made myself vulnerable, and explained to my advisor that I was stressed by not understanding the fees. I asked that he show me, by way of comparison to other investment houses, that he was competitive. My advisor was happy to do it and commended me for attempting to deepen my engagement with my finances.

I'm not the only business person who's found Byron Katie's The Work invaluable. Derek Bullen is the founder and president of Calgary-based S.i. Systems, one of the largest staffing firms in North America. Bullen attended a workshop on The Work, given by my friend, Dr. Lara Patriquin. After the workshop was over, he was so impressed by the clarity he gained in a personal situation that he decided to pull a team of his high potential employees together and had Dr. Patriquin and her colleagues at an organization called Innerland teach them how to do The Work. Within a few months, he told me, these managers were having deeper conversations and making clearer decisions. There were even several promotions as a result. As Bullen described, "Our conversations are now much more factual and the tempo of resolving and addressing issues is much faster... Managers tend to get presented with results or excuses and The Work allows us to inquire into these excuses. Now we ask, 'Is that true?' a lot more."

When I asked Bullen about how The Work had had an impact on his professional life, he told me a story of an accounting issue that had been kept secret from him for four years. "It was a huge mess," he said, "eleven-and-a-half million dollars was unaccounted for." He was bitter, angry, and resentful about the situation and was holding on tightly to these negative thoughts and feelings. It was only after doing The Work that he made peace with what happened and was grateful for the opportunity it offered. The turnarounds helped him to see that the situation was a gift in that it gave him the impetus to bring on a new CFO and completely overhaul the accounting team. The Work also shifted his anger around the lost money. First, he had to acknowledge that most of the money had been found and accounted for and, second, he was holding onto the large figure as his "truth," as opposed to the actual amount of lost money, which was more like three million. Rational thinking prevailed and he was able to let go of the stress.

✦

I HAD AN opportunity to ask Byron Katie why The Work is effective for high achieving, ambitious people. She replied, "The mind that is free is open to many possibilities. When high achieving people learn how to question their stressful thoughts, they find that conflicts begin to disappear. This leads to greater efficiency and frees up immense creative energy. Inner peace is a very attractive quality." A free mind, an open mind, is what I wanted. Irrational thinking, evident in our cognitive biases, can become a mental prison, but only if we let it. Believing my theories kept me blind to the truth, which is exactly what happened with Hanson and his dog and with my financial advisor. Byron Katie's The Work offered me a road map to the truth, though not without some intense labour on my part.

Now when I think about being a prisoner of my thoughts, one specific image comes to mind. When Chris and I were in Florence during our trip around the world, we lined up at the Galleria dell'Accademia to see the famous statue of David. But it was another Michelangelo masterpiece that captured my attention—the Prisoner sculptures. Michelangelo had started carving a series of nudes out of blocks of marble but the sculptures had not been completed. As a result, the sculptures look like people still caught inside marble blocks, fighting for release. I was ready to break free from my marble block.

If I could free myself from my own thought patterns, perhaps the sun that I saw shining faintly in my own focus group would get a little brighter. I had no idea that it would only take a few more weeks before I was positively blinded.

Chapter 5

WHO HAS TIME TO BE PRESENT?

CURIOSITY IS A visceral feeling for me. When I realize I have stumbled across something I was previously unaware of, it feels like a surge of electric current. Sometimes, the desire to know more turns into hunger, a longing or yearning. Four months into my mesearch project with Ean, I described this feeling as "insatiable." Every morning I woke up wondering what I would discover about myself that day as opposed to my typical thoughts: can I skip swim practice? and oh God, when can I sleep next?

My curiosity did not do much to cool my achiever fever, however. In fact, by this point I had already begun to experience some fever around understanding the fever. For example, I didn't see myself as being just four months into my project, but rather as having only eight months left to learn. What if the project didn't work? What if a year wasn't enough? Hurry and worry, two key achiever fever attributes, which handily trump the slow deliciousness of curiosity.

Since my twenties, so much in my life has felt rushed. Rushing to finish something, rushing to check something off, rushing to learn something, rushing to get back to someone, rushing to get somewhere, rushing to accomplish something. And, if I'm not hurrying, I'm worrying about getting it all done. For as long as I can remember, life has been about what comes next. I'll be happy when... I'll feel better when... I can chill out when... I can't wait until..., Believing that there was always something that needed to be completed by a specific time, even on a rainy Sunday afternoon, made planning an important part of my life.

As a business owner, it is my job to plan strategy, budget, and resources. When we're in first quarter, I'm thinking about third quarter; when we're in third quarter, I'm thinking about next fiscal. Before I've even climbed out of bed, I check my phone to see what's on my agenda for the day. When I get to my desk, I make a list of what needs to be done. I use my inbox as my general to-do list, which means every email represents a task I need to accomplish. I remember my dad once telling me to start my day by tackling the task I least wanted to do—great advice I've never followed. On the weekends, I make a list of chores that need to get done (buy new bedding, clean out kitchen cupboards, get in x number of workouts), get overwhelmed, and spend the next two hours reading the newspaper on the couch feeling guilty.

During my insomniac days in Seattle, I took planning to the extreme. I needed to be on the highway before seven every morning to avoid rush hour traffic and get a swim workout in at the gym close to my work. Each night, I would pack my swim gear, my work clothes, my lunch, and a couple of snacks. To avoid the traffic on the homebound commute, I would often go to the climbing gym after work, so I had to pack all my climbing gear as well. Each morning I would wake up rushing to get on the road and that feeling stayed with me all day.

At work, my eye was constantly on the clock—fitting in project planning, meetings, proposal writing, and budget planning. If I had a ten-minute window between meetings, I would use that time to book a personal appointment or read an article. Twenty-minute windows were built into my week to call my family. Everything became a list item to check off. As soon as something was complete, another task would replace it. Exhausted at the end of the day, I'd pour a large glass of wine, watch a blissful hour or two of a favourite TV show, and then get into bed. As I lay there I'd be planning the next day, and the day after that, and then the next trip to see Chris, and our trip around the world, and the next five years of our life. Of course I had insomnia! I haven't experienced that level of intensity since Seattle but I have remained a planner.

Amplifying this future orientation of mine is that the market research industry largely exists to predict the future. Survey data is used by clients to either get a handle on what may happen in the upcoming months or years, or to provide them with benchmark numbers so they have something to compare future results with. But trying to predict the future is how many businesses operate. Any number of business clichés point to this obsession: "focus on the future," "grow or die," and the ubiquitous, "at the end of the day."

Living for the future comes so naturally to achievers. As goal setters, we tend to keep our eyes on the finish line, which means everything becomes a step towards the goal. This is one of the reasons I started the mesearch project—my life was passing me by in a flurry of "to do" lists. Surely, other people weren't this caught up in the future? My achiever survey proved me wrong. Seventy percent of achievers said that they tend to focus more on the future than they do on the present. Yet they keep doing it at the cost of enjoying what is happening right in front of them. My learning to backcountry ski is a good example of this.

I grew up on the Canadian prairies where the land is so flat that the joke goes you can watch your dog run away for days. Not surprisingly, I never learned to downhill ski. But when I moved to the West Coast, however, it seemed everyone knew how to ski. It wasn't until I met Chris and moved back to Vancouver that I decided to learn. Chris, and most of our friends, were expert skiers and had spent time backcountry skiing, which meant hiking up steep inclines with skins on the bottom of their skis so that they could lay down fresh tracks down the other side. No chair lifts, just miles of fresh powder. If I wanted to spend time with Chris on winter weekends, I needed to learn how to do this. My goal was never "learn how to ski," but rather, "ski well in the backcountry."

I took a few lessons at a local resort and spent a couple of years skiing groomed hills. I didn't enjoy this because I was always lagging far behind my friends. Making it worse was my conviction that skiing was something I was innately bad at because it was "not in my blood." I was so focused on progressing to more difficult hills that I didn't get comfortable with speed. Fear would stop me several times down a run. Of course, the more fear I felt the more the Judge screamed at me to try harder. I also attacked myself for not enjoying the sport that everyone else seemed to love so much.

I took an avalanche course I barely understood and eventually got out in the backcountry. Gone was the safety of the resort, and now I had to learn how to ski around trees and read the runs, all in steep powder. Because I fell so often, I was constantly digging myself out of deep snow, which was exhausting. I couldn't shake the constant fear that I was either going to ski into a tree or ski off the side of the mountain, and I was embarrassed by being so much slower than everyone else. One day, about three months after starting my program with Ean, I completely lost it on a group trip in the Whistler backcountry. There were about eight of us skiing and I had fallen midway down the run, lost a ski, and was buried so deep in powder I clocked the thought, well, I guess this is it for me. Chris skied over to check on me, as he had countless times before, but this time I could not impress him with my fake go-getter cheerfulness. Instead, at the top of my lungs, I screamed, "Fuck this! I fucking hate this shit!" As my cursing reverberated throughout the pristine winter wilderness, Chris, who would normally try to soothe my exasperation by praising me, looked me right in the eyes and hissed, "Stop it. You are acting like a child." Now shame and humiliation was mixed in with my anger, especially when I realized the rest of the group, at the bottom of the run, had heard me yelling.

"I just want to be good at skiing," I moaned to Ean the next day. "I want to get to the point where I actually enjoy it!"

"How long have you been skiing?" Ean asked.

"Almost four years!" I said.

"How long have your friends been skiing?" he asked next.

I thought about it for a couple of seconds. I sighed, realizing what he was getting at. "Most of their lives," I admitted.

Again, I was rushing to be good at something; rushing so I could enjoy skiing—because it would only be enjoyable when I was good at it. Ean encouraged me to stop comparing myself with these other expert skiers and accept that I was still learning. Then he said something that I was finally ready to hear. He told me to enjoy the learning for the simple pleasure of learning. By taking the goal out of the equation, I would have a much better time and probably learn faster in the process. Throwing myself at the finish line was not serving me. I was logging time, rather than living time, and robbing myself of the experience of learning to ski.

As I drove home after our session, I realized how deep this pattern of rushing ran within me. I liked activities that I excelled at naturally, like swimming and climbing. But when I couldn't get from A to B fast enough, I'd disparage the activity and myself. I did this with my PhD, with guitar lessons, and even with trying to get pregnant for the ten months I'd decided to make it a goal. How did that line go? A means to an end. I was all about the ends. Means were something just to get through. If, as Ean was saying, the joy was in the learning, it made sense that I hadn't experienced a lot of joy. The achievements felt good, but the giddiness of achieving the goal was always over so quickly. And goals were replaced by new goals. In fact, it was in recognizing that meeting my professional and personal goals had not led to the happiness I assumed they would that brought me to Ean in the first place.

Ninety percent of achievers in my survey said they are happiest when they achieve their goals, but I was sick of tying my happiness to my achievements. What if I could stop relying on achievements to make me happy and instead find happiness on the way? The concept seemed too foreign to contemplate. Then three things happened to make the notion seem less outlandish.

✦

I ROLLED MY eyes when I first signed up for it, but Kung Fu first introduced me to what happens when we let go of the future. I had been taking Kung Fu every Wednesday since the beginning of that year, but the name alone seemed so ridiculous that I couldn't tell anyone about it. Plus, like skiing, I was way behind everyone else in my class—I was the newest student, and, for the first time that I could remember, the oldest. Of course, like anything else in my life, I wanted to be good at it.

Within a few months, I had learned how to throw a decent punch, a whole series of kicks and combinations, and even memorized a form, which are a series of several kicks and punches strung together. I earned my white belt and was staggered by my ability to do something I was initially convinced looked impossible. As I became more comfortable, I started to enjoy it and even began talking to friends about it and showing Chris my moves in our living room. The comfort did not last long.

One Wednesday, Ean told us that we were going to start sparring and that we'd need to buy gear. I went to a martial arts store and purchased shin pads, gloves, and headgear. I was excited to see what sparring was about. A few weeks later at class, we put on our gear and waited for instructions. Ean explained that it was time to start using the kicks and punches on each other. He emphasized that the goal was just a light touch to the opponent—this was not about throwing hard punches. He taught us to keep our hands up to protect our faces as we circled our opponent and to look for openings to land a light punch on their head or torso.

I watched a couple of the other students spar, looking for areas that were open and touching their opponent with their glove or shin. Everyone was very respectful. The rounds were only a minute in length and seemed to race by. I could feel myself getting nervous; would I be able to do this? Too quickly, it was my turn. My opponent was a girl named Tiff, short for Tiffany. She had started Kung Fu only a few months before me but was committed and practiced diligently. I liked and was inspired by her.

Ean put a minute on the clock and Tiff and I touched gloves. We pulled back and began circling each other as Ean called out, "Keep your hands up." Tiff came at me first, landing a soft touch to the side of my head. I threw one back and missed entirely. The fact that she was a foot taller than me was suddenly very apparent. I realized I needed to be more strategic but that thought was obliterated by a punch that came at me, again at the side of my head. I immediately reacted by throwing one myself, this time connecting with the side of her stomach. She then got me twice in a row, again in the head.

I was breathing hard by this point, trying to stay out of her way while trying to land a punch at the same time. I was punching a lot of air. My chest was tight, my hands were all over the place, and I had stopped breathing. Tiff landed another punch. I was getting frustrated. She got the side of my head. I was getting mad. She got me again. Ok, this was not fun. I looked over at the clock, expecting to see that the round was up but saw that only thirty seconds had elapsed. How was that possible? Desperation kicked in as Tiff landed a couple more punches. I was now more focused on trying to stay away from her, throwing one punch for every three or four she threw. I heard Ean encouraging me to stay close and go for it, but I was dropping back, throwing weak punches, mentally pleading for this to be over. I was exhausted. Then, just before the buzzer went, Tiff got me on my forehead. It was just a light tap, but to me, it felt like the knockout blow. Involuntarily, my hands went up in defeat.

Tears began to prickle in my eyes and I clenched my face trying to hold them at bay. I was over a decade older than the other students. I would not cry. I would not cry. But the tears came. Mortified, I ran out of the room. We practiced in Ean's basement, so I stumbled up the stairs and ended up in the kitchen. I leaned against his oven and cried. I was so embarrassed and disgusted with myself. I so desperately wanted to leave, to get in my car, and never, ever come back. Ean soon came up the stairs and handed me some tissue. He said, "It's OK, just let it out. Don't do anything but cry for two minutes. Then watch yourself and see what happens."

Now that I had permission to cry, I let it all out. Ugly-face sobbing. The Judge was on my case immediately: "You are such a loser! All this time with Ean and you haven't learned anything. What are you even doing here at Kung Fu anyway? You're terrible at it! And this is how you handle yourself?"

I cried harder—I wasn't improving at all. Everything I'd done with Ean had been a complete waste of time. I looked up at the clock on the wall. Ean had told me to cry for a couple of minutes and I still had a minute left. The hard sobbing had ended and I was wiping my nose and sniffling but I still had a minute to go. Based on my sparring round, I knew how long a minute could last. So, I continued to lean against his oven, wiping my tears and watching the clock. Within a few seconds, I noticed my breath calming down and everything seemed to slow down. I took some deep breaths and suddenly became aware of a physical pull, like someone was standing beside me, trying to drag me sideways out of the room and towards the front door. I shut my eyes and heard my thoughts clearly.

I'm a climber and a swimmer, I don't need to do this.
I'm an adult, I don't have to be here.
No one is paying me to do this.
I want to leave, I want to quit and drive away.

Though I was cognizant of thinking these thoughts, I made no move to leave. It was like there were two of us. The one who was mortified and desperate to get out of the house and the one watching this happen. I opened my eyes and saw the clock, the white fridge, and the tissue in my hand. Everything slowed to a crawl. I wasn't trying to plan what I would say or do. I wasn't replaying the sparring. I was just there in Ean's kitchen. Suddenly I felt very clear. The thought about jumping in my car to drive away had passed and I hadn't given in to it. The real sparring had just happened in Ean's kitchen. I had taken on doubt, fear, anger, frustration, and humiliation, and won. I was ready to go back downstairs.

As I entered the room, everyone turned towards me and I could feel their compassion—no one was judging me. Tiff immediately came up and said, "I'm so sorry, I feel terrible." I gave her a hug, assured her she had done nothing wrong, thanked her for inspiring me, and meant it. I admitted to the group that I was embarrassed but that I was fine, and said it with a smile on my face. There was nothing fake about this cool sense of calm I was feeling. I told them how surprised I had been by my reaction, but that I was glad it had happened because it had given me an opportunity to see myself up close and personal.

By this point the practice had ended and as I got in my car, I noticed that the calm feeling continued to stay with me. A few minutes into the drive, I caught myself singing along to the radio. I was happy, really happy. Joyful, in fact. I knew it had something to do with this feeling of having a staring contest with myself and not looking away. Was this what it meant to get out of my own way?

When I talked about it the next morning with Ean, he explained that by watching myself, as I leaned against his oven, I was experiencing being present. This gave me the ability to see my thoughts as they occurred and kept me from giving into the impulse to flee. The Judge wanted me to run. I simply watched it talk. Rather than acting on my thoughts, I had watched them. This was why time had slowed down. The clarity, the calm, the appreciation for myself and others, Ean said, was the result of staying present. It's in moments of awareness like this, Ean said, that you are alive to what is happening right now. "Being present in your life," he explained, "will bring you the peace, the fulfilment, the joy you're looking for."

Until the Kung Fu experience, I was the first to judge if I heard someone use phrases like "be in the moment" or "be present"— these words had always struck me as saccharine. Moreover, they simply weren't attainable. I would think, who has time to be present? If I was driving to a meeting, I would think about what I might say at that meeting. If I was having a conversation, I would think about what I would say next. If I was doing sit-ups at the end of my workout, I would think about what to have for breakfast and what to wear to work and what I would make for dinner. So many thoughts upon thoughts—my brain never had room for a moment of so-called presence.

But that moment in Ean's kitchen had shown me what happens when we stay with the present moment and simply notice, or become aware, of what is happening. In only a few minutes of watching my thoughts and emotions, I had not only overcome the impulse to flee but moved from mortification to acceptance to courage to happiness. What if I applied this approach in other areas of my life?

Like most people, I love my phone. I see it as a constant source of potential good news, like a lottery ticket. Usually the messages are mundane: sorry, try again. But occasionally, the message is a jackpot, like a new project win, an invite to a cool event, a speaking request. My phone also helped me feel plugged in and in control. I'd heard colleagues say they were addicted to their phones but never thought that of myself. I'd also heard the media stories about traffic accidents being caused by distracted drivers. I was not immune to the pleas by the police to stop driving and texting, but I still kept my phone on the passenger seat so I could check it at red lights. Illegal though it was, I rationalized that I was only checking it when my car was stopped.

One afternoon I was driving to Kung Fu. It was around five so work emails were still flying. I pulled up at a red light and took my hand off the wheel to grab my phone. But as my hand reached for it, I caught myself in the act. With my hand in mid-air, I noticed how strong the urge was to pick up the phone. It was a shocking feeling: I *needed* that phone. It reminded me of that powerful physical pull I had felt to leave in Ean's kitchen, and, in that moment, with my hand suspended in the air, I decided to simply watch my thoughts. It was like I was hovering over my own body watching my reaction. I became aware of a few emotions: I felt angry because I was not allowing myself to do something. I felt desperate—like something bad might happen if I didn't check it, something could go wrong and it was all up to me to make sure nothing bad happened. I also noticed I felt frustrated because there was a potential treat on the phone and I was keeping myself from it. My hand still in the air, I physically shook my head, amazed at how strong these thoughts and emotions were. No wonder checking my phone was so addictive, no wonder I found it so difficult to not give into the impulse. It was only a few seconds before the light turned green but, as I drove away, I experienced the same feeling of winning a staring contest with myself. I had wanted, needed, to pick up the phone but, by not blindly acting on the impulse, I had seen my phone addiction up close and personal. I felt empowered, but I also felt that same calm, cool peacefulness I had felt at Ean's. And it led to an immediate behavioural change. To this day, I haven't checked my phone in my car.

I had learned, experientially, what happened when one stayed present and had seen the enormous power in it. But how could I sustain this level of awareness? When I asked Ean about this, he recommended that I check out an author named Eckhart Tolle. Tolle, Ean said, was probably a different kind of author than I was used to. He was not a psychologist, journalist, or business writer. Rather, Ean explained, Tolle offered an unconventional approach to life worth my exploration.

The next day I went on a search for Eckhart Tolle's book. When I asked the book clerk to show me where it was, she walked me deep into the store, pointed it out, and left me—in the Self-Help section. Oh shit. I didn't do self-help. I glanced at the covers and grimaced—a bunch of moony-looking people talking about motivation, positivity, deities, and diets. And there, in the middle of it all, was Tolle's book, *The Power of Now*.

The book's yellow and blue pastel marbled cover immediately reminded me of those "Footprints in the Sand" posters I grew up seeing in dentists' offices. Checking to see that no one was looking, I picked it up. The text at the top of the cover told me it was a *New York Times* bestseller and a starburst informed me that several million copies had been sold. Underneath the title was the subheading *A Guide to Spiritual Enlightenment.* I left the store, bought it on my e-reader instead, and started reading the next day.

Eckhart Tolle introduces himself by saying that up until the third decade of his life, he lived in a near constant state of anxiety and depression. The thing he hated most was himself. One morning, out of the blue, Tolle woke up with the realization that nothing in life was causing his suffering. He had no diseases, he wasn't starving, he had a home, his basic needs were met. This recognition, he says, completely transformed him. In suddenly understanding that he had been suffering for no reason, all his fear, self-doubt, and anger simply fell away. He woke up.

As I read, I remember feeling skeptical but also a yearning to know more. Tolle writes about the pain of struggling with self-doubt, anger, fear, guilt, and self-loathing. He writes about the voice in our heads that, in his words, torments and attacks us. He explains that all human beings suffer from it. Soon I was speed reading, curiosity coursing through me.

Tolle also explains that the misery and pain we all feel is caused by our thoughts. In fact, most of what Tolle writes about is thoughts. Not his personal thoughts, not types of thoughts, just thoughts. I'd never thought about thoughts as a thing before. Human beings have thoughts like we have lungs, ears, and arms. We don't think about the fact that we have thoughts, they are just part of what makes us human. Descartes famously summed it up by saying "I think, therefore I am." But thinking, Tolle argues, is the problem. Thinking creates pain and despair and keeps us either in the past or the future. Thoughts build on previous thoughts. They are anchored in what has already happened, and so keep us in the past. (Hello left-brain interpreter.)

Sometimes we experience this as thinking about what has happened, what was said, what should have been said. Some of us will get caught up with thoughts of regret. Alternatively, we are thinking about the future or projecting ahead. This was certainly the case for me and for most of my surveyed achievers—with seventy percent agreeing they tend to focus more on the future than they do on the present. And what happens when we think about the future? We worry. Some of us, including three quarters of the surveyed female achievers, worry a lot.

If I added up the amount of time I had spent worrying, it would surely equate to years of my life. Not a "wringing my hands" worry, though there had been plenty of that, but worrying about what might happen, worrying about what could go wrong, worrying I had said the wrong thing, worrying that I had made a bad decision.

This feeling of worry had been my normal for so long that I would even worry about worrying. On vacations, I would worry about how much time I had left, anxious to make the remaining days worry-free. Then I would recognize that by being consumed by the worry, I wouldn't enjoy the actual vacation. Then I would worry about not enjoying it and then worry about worrying about not enjoying it. Worrying hurts because it tends to involve imagining worst-case scenarios, or, as a friend of mine calls it, catastrophizing. Tolle's book brought to mind a bumper sticker I had once seen: "Worrying is praying for what you don't want."

Tolle had spent years worrying, years imagining all the bad things that could happen. But when he woke up one morning at twenty-nine, he realized that none of those things that he worried about had happened and probably wouldn't happen. He was living in a state of fear that he had manufactured through his thinking. It was not reality. He was delusional, just like me. Just like, he argues, all of us.

Worrying had kept me trapped in a world that does not exist. When I coupled my tendency to worry with my tendency to assume that things would be better in the future, I saw the complete disconnect in my thinking. How could the future be where all the worries took place, but, at the same time, be the promised land when I would finally be happy?

As I was reading Tolle's book, I had an experience that helped bring this conundrum to life. As a sessional instructor at a university, I was often invited out to student events. As I got ready to attend an evening's talk by a local entrepreneur, I had the same thought I had in similar situations many times before—I just gotta get through this. It had been a long day and I was tired. I was going out of duty to the students. Once the event was over, I would go home, put on my pyjamas, lie on my couch, and watch something on TV—this was what I was thinking about as I caught a cab to the event.

Upon arriving, I said hello to my students, grabbed a glass of wine, and waited for the speaker to get started. He droned on for a bit about starting his company and what he had learned in the process. And then he said something interesting. He said that when he himself listened to other speakers, he went to those events with an intention to learn. Prior to the event, he would say to himself, "What am I going to get from this speaker tonight?" The line echoed in my head. I suddenly saw myself with my glass of wine in the darkened room. I came to these events to get through them. He came to get from them. My thinking was framed by wanting the event to be over. His thinking was framed by wanting to learn. I was thinking about what would come next. He would be listening to what was being said. He was present and learning. Meanwhile, I had wasted another evening of my life.

At that moment, Tolle's title, *The Power of Now,* suddenly made a lot of sense. Between the "getting through it," the worrying, the scheduling, the time-boxing, the projecting, the planning, the imagining, the daydreams of "I'll be happy when," I was never experiencing the present moment or what Tolle calls "The Now." When we are present, when we give something one hundred percent of our attention, the more alive we feel, and the more joy we feel. Tolle argues that being "in the now" is the prerequisite to truly experiencing and enjoying our lives. Was this what would make me the happy and confident person I so badly wanted to be? If so, how? Thankfully, Tolle offers some advice.

When he was in the grip of depression and anxiety, Tolle often thought the following phrase: "I cannot live with myself any longer." But one day, after thinking that, something occurred to him: "Am I one or two? If I cannot live with myself, there must be two of me: the 'I' and the 'self' that 'I' cannot live with. Maybe, I thought, only one of them is real."[16]

Upon first reading his words, I had three thoughts. The first was, "Huh? That makes zero sense." But it kept my curiosity intrigued. The second thought, "I could no longer live with myself," sounded similar to my own thought loop, "I've got to get out of my own way." The third thought was that I had already experienced this "two people one body" thing in the discovery of the Judge. If the Judge was talking, how can I be listening? How can this be happening at the same time?

Though I was confused, I intuited that Tolle was telling me something important. What we need to do, he says, is "watch the thinker." The thinker is the manufacturer of thoughts and we can watch those thoughts being manufactured. This is exactly what Ean had wanted me to do in the kitchen—watch myself. Tolle encourages us to watch the thinker as often as we can, but the only way we are able to do this is by staying present. Once we can watch the thinker, we see how controlled we are by our thoughts and see the pain that results.

Watching the Judge with my one to four numbering system had given me a good foundation for watching the thinker. However, I quickly learned that watching the thinker was much more difficult. To do it, one needs the desire to do it in the first place, an openness to the idea that watching one's thoughts is possible, and infinite patience to practice it.

For the next few weeks, I'd wake up and remind myself to watch my thoughts. Then I'd instantly forget. The reminder would come when I suddenly clued into the fact that I was brushing my teeth, checking my phone, packing my yoga gear, and looking for my sunglasses all at the same time. Stop! I would tell myself. Remember! Be present! Watch your thoughts! Then I would see the time, realize I was running late, and forget again. Later in the evening, I would again be reminded when I saw I was unstacking the dishwasher, sending a text, changing the song I was listening to, glancing at an article in the newspaper lying on the island, grabbing food from the fridge—all within the space of about thirty seconds. When I became aware of what I was doing, I would finally stop and see that my thoughts were so rushed and plentiful I could hardly keep up with them, let alone watch them. When this happened, I'd sigh in frustration, recognize I was getting mad at myself, shake my head, smile, and start again. And again. And again. This became a pattern for the next few weeks.

Part of the delight of catching a thought was that I knew I was present in that moment. It is impossible to catch a thought unless one is present. And catching thoughts makes one present. Understanding this, I tried to become more focused on doing one thing at a time. When I brushed my teeth, I brushed my teeth. When I unstacked the dishwasher, I unstacked the dishwasher. This helped slow my thoughts down and I could watch them a little more easily.

Sometimes, when I became aware I was on autopilot, I would take a deep breath and notice what was happening around me. I would feel peaceful for a couple of seconds until the moment was interrupted by a barrage of thoughts about what I had to do next. Occasionally, as I talked with co-workers, I would be aware that my mind was formulating what to say in response. Whenever I caught myself doing this, I'd stop, take a breath, and focus on the other person. Suddenly, I'd physically feel a warmer, deeper connection with them, but it would evaporate in a couple of seconds when the next thought came along. These tiny present moments were lovely but they were so few and far between.

One Sunday afternoon, about five months into the mesearch project, I was in the kitchen chopping vegetables. This was something I had begun doing that year with Ean, prepping my food for the week by slicing cabbage, grating carrots and beets, dicing celery, and shredding kale. I'd put all the prepped vegetables in plastic tubs in my fridge so that I could grab handfuls to take for lunch each day. I loved those chopping sessions. I'd turn on my music and focus on my knife. The methodical slicing and grating calmed my thoughts. It was a great way to practice being present, fully in The Now. I was also reminded of what my friend Dr. Lara Patriquin had said about a flow state quieting the left-brain interpreter. Between the music and the slicing and dicing, I was indeed in a flow. My mind was quiet allowing me to be aware of thoughts as they crept up.

That afternoon, I was listening to Phosphorescent's "Song For Zula," and, as I chopped cabbage, tears suddenly sprang to my eyes. I was surprised. I hadn't been thinking of anything to make me sad. But I didn't have any time to think anything else because suddenly tears were pouring down my face, and I had to grab the side of the kitchen island to steady myself. I knew enough at this point to just watch, not think. And I recognized that these were not tears of sadness, these were tears of pure joy. My stomach seized as I realized I was experiencing something new, something that I couldn't explain, and I gave myself over to this feeling flowing through me. Welcoming it rather than questioning it intensified the experience, and I was sobbing and laughing at the same time. Then, I was overcome, completely overcome, with gratitude. In that moment, completely in The Now, I was unbelievably thankful for my life. For Chris. For my family. For my music. For my kitchen. For my food. For this project. For myself.

The whole thing lasted for about four minutes. I watched my mind trying to make sense of what was happening while at the same time knowing it didn't matter. As the tears came to an end, a feeling of deep peace settled over me. I grabbed my journal and tried to replicate in words what I just felt. I couldn't do the feeling justice, I still can't. But I had a feeling that what had happened was something that Tolle talks about. He says that glimpses of pure, overwhelming joy can be felt when one is perfectly present, when everything is still and there is a gap in our thoughts. I didn't care if the trigger for the experience was the song, a quiet mind, or the cabbage. All I knew is that I had experienced something I had never felt before and it was beautiful. There was no achievement, no striving. No accomplishment had ever made me feel like this.

Around that time, I recall seeing a visual of a trapeze in someone's conference presentation. It occurred to me that I was the acrobat leaving the safe familiarity of one bar to grab another. I felt like I was in mid-air. A little scared and unsettled but also bursting with a desire to grab on to the next and discover more.

On that Sunday afternoon, I had experienced a tiny, tiny fraction of what was available if I was to learn to stay present. If this was how being in The Now made me feel, I wanted more of it.

Chapter 6

MESEARCH

"I GOTTA GO to the bathroom," Chris said. "I'll be right back."

It was eight in the morning and we'd just finished packing up the tent. We had camped beside the highway and were ready to begin our multi-day hike in the mountains. The weather was perfect with a bright blue sky and enough breeze that the hike wouldn't be too hot. Our backpacks sat in the backseat, everything organized and ready for when we arrived at the trailhead.

I was in the passenger seat of Chris's car. An early morning bathroom break meant a short hike into the woods, and I probably had a good fifteen minutes before he came back. As he headed out, I felt the familiar urge to check my phone, but it was buried deep in my pack so it wouldn't get wet if it rained. My next thought was to grab my book, but it too was carefully packed. With no phone and no book, I had nothing to do. A mild panic crept up in my stomach—the prospect of boredom loomed. Noticing the feeling, I shifted into observing my thoughts and behaviour. I watched myself glance around the car for something to keep me occupied. Chris had taken the keys so I couldn't listen to the radio. I opened the glove compartment looking for a pen so I could at least describe how important it seemed to me to fill this empty space. No pen, so I watched myself reach for the car manual. May as well use the time to learn something. A few minutes into reading about the engine light, I put the book down and shook my head. Holy shit. Is this really who I am?

Nothing to do. The promise of it always seems so delicious—lying on a beach or swinging in a hammock with absolutely nothing to do. How many times had I thought or even said aloud, "I can't wait till I have absolutely nothing to do." But when those moments presented themselves, like it did on the side of the road before our hike, I got anxious. Having nothing to do felt like idleness, which made me feel lazy, which made me feel guilty. Usually, when I found unplanned time in my day, my first thought was that I'd forgotten to do something. Either way, my belief was that time was there to be filled, not wasted, and this need to feel productive stoked my achiever fever.

My go-to tool to ensure I never felt at loose ends, bored, or lonely is a book. It is the perfect combination of productive entertainment. When I was a kid, I used to bring my clock radio into bed so I could read under the covers. For my honeymoon, I brought a big stack of books with me. The first feature I look for in a purse is that it is big enough to hold a book. When I am in complete despair, it is almost always a book that brings me back to life. I once heard a story about someone shipwrecked on a desert island. The only thing he had to read was the label on a soup can so he buried it to keep himself from devouring the words. Each day, he'd dig it up, allow himself one word, then bury it again. That would be me.

In my house I have a piece of furniture I call my "content couch." One of my favourite things to do was to sit on that couch surrounded by content. On a rainy Saturday afternoon, you'd find me curled up there with the following: the novel I was currently reading as well as the novel I would read next, a couple of library books, the thick weekend edition of the newspaper, the newest issue of the *Atlantic Monthly*, a tablet containing another magazine I was working through, like *Outside* or *Vanity Fair*. My phone would be on the armrest so I could easily respond to texts or look something up. My laptop would usually be at my feet so I could check email. Swimming in pages and screens, this was my happiest place. Such beautiful irony then that I would learn the value and importance of doing nothing while sitting on my content couch.

Six months into my work with Ean and learning so much from Eckhart Tolle's book, my appetite for similar books was voracious. I gravitated to memoirs in the same section of the bookstore (I couldn't bring myself to use the words "spiritual" or "self-help") about people like me who were sick and tired of feeling sick and tired and had learned what I was learning: how to observe the voice in their heads, watch their thoughts, and the importance of living in the present moment.

I read *Be Here Now* by Ram Dass, a psychologist at Harvard in the sixties who worked down the hall from Timothy Leary. Hugely successful but desperately unhappy, Ram Dass craved change. Between taking hallucinogens (his book is full of trippy graphics and illustrations) and multiple lengthy trips to India, he became aware that it was his thoughts that had manufactured a false reality. Like Tolle, the title of his book is his antidote.

The *Way of the Peaceful Warrior* by Dan Millman resonated strongly with me because Millman was the ultimate Type-A personality: a scholarship athlete, a martial artist, and a world champion gymnast. He was also a world-class sufferer of achiever fever. Utterly unhappy, Millman was initially convinced that self-improvement would help him. He, too, learned that fulfillment cannot be found in the "fixing," but in the sharpening of one's mind. These authors, and others like them, such as Dan Harris in his book *10% Happier*, use words like path and journey in their stories. I couldn't help but see that these words, as hippie-dippie as they may have sounded, might also apply to me. And for the first time I felt a flutter of awareness that this research project might have an extended timeline.

Another thing that these authors talked a lot about was meditation. In fact, meditation came up in almost every book, article, blog post, podcast, and documentary I was consuming. Meditation, an ancient spiritual practice, has been proven effective in increasing mental and physical well-being. And thousands of scientific studies prove that it is beneficial in the reduction of stress. Sara Lazar, a neuroscientist at Harvard Medical School, tested the benefits of meditation using brain scans. Long-term meditators were shown to have increased grey matter in sensory regions, which meant a heightened experience of the world around them. Her research also showed increased grey matter in the frontal cortex, an area associated with decision-making. Rather than getting carried away with the tens of thousands of thoughts that cross our brains each day, meditation enhances one's ability to focus, a useful thing for multi-tasking achievers. Lazar's studies also showed that only eight weeks of consistent meditation could reduce anxiety, fear, and stress as a result of its impact on the amygdala, the fight or flight part of the brain.[17]

Along with anxiety, meditation has been shown to improve depression and insomnia with some studies going so far as to say meditation is as effective as antidepressants.[18] Even the Harvard Business Journal was running articles on the usefulness of meditation for CEOs, calling it out as a critical tool for boosting effective decision-making, mood, and resilience.

I knew intellectually that meditation was useful for helping you to stay present, something I could not deny the power of, and that it was supposed to strengthen your ability to listen to your intuition, rather than get caught up in the wandering mind. Other articles talked about meditation as a tool for increasing self-compassion, something I knew I lacked.

Meditation was making its way into companies as well. One day, I was attending a meeting at one of our clients, a natural foods company called Nature's Path. At noon, an announcement came over the PA, calling all interested employees to a noon meditation session. I was shocked—here it was being offered in my own backyard.

All the signposts were directing me toward meditation. But the trouble was, I didn't want to do it. Decades of avoiding being alone with my thoughts had made the prospect of actively choosing to do so unimaginable. Used to learning from secondary sources likes books and people like Ean, I much preferred to read about meditation than practice it. Back then, I didn't understand how meditation necessarily made me my own teacher.

✦

IN THE MARKET research industry, there is a type of research called ethnography, a term co-opted from anthropologists.

Ethnography means studying research participants in their natural habitat, whether that is in their homes, their workplaces, or even grocery stores. Ethnography allows researchers to watch participants' decisions and behaviours in real time. We also call it "fly on the wall" research or research "close to the vine." Just like the freshest fruit are those on the vine, the freshest insights come from direct observation.

With some surprise I realized that what I had been doing for the past six months was conducting ethnography on myself, a sort of autoethnography. I looked it up on Wikipedia to see if the term existed. Autoethnography was indeed a thing: "a form of qualitative research in which an author uses self-reflection and writing to explore their personal experience and connect this autobiographical story to wider cultural, political, and social meanings and understandings."[19] Though the second part of this description didn't apply at the time, the self-reflection and journaling through my work with Ean held true. And, although my interior barrier to meditation was powerful, intuitively I knew it was the best way to practice autoethnography and was the perfect mesearch methodology.

I put it off for as long as possible. When I thought about meditating, I visualized myself in a painful cross-legged position, boring myself to death. Why would I want to sit there, doing absolutely nothing, when I had so much to get done? Plus, I knew just thirty seconds would bring up the Judge, who would be screaming: "You're wasting your time, you should be working." No thanks. But mostly, I was scared. Scared about what might bubble up in my mind just sitting there, thoughts that may be scary, thoughts about my past, my ex-husband, stuff I just didn't want to know or think about. I was also scared that I wouldn't be able to do it. All these authors I had been reading didn't just meditate—they were meditators. What if I couldn't do it? Would I go back to my old life of fear, self-doubt, and unhappiness? Better not to know.

My attitude towards meditation is commonplace among achievers even though many of them perceive meditation as a useful practice. Sixty percent of the self-identified achievers in my survey said they wished they had a meditation practice or that they were curious to try it. About fifteen percent said they have no personal interest, but only two percent saw it as a waste of time. What keeps achievers from engaging in meditation? Twenty percent of female achievers said they didn't have enough time, while others were more specific. One achiever said, "I keep myself busy and distracted so I don't have to go into my head alone." Another said, "I worry it will be something I try and that either it doesn't work or that I fail at it and it becomes one more thing I didn't achieve." Both comments applied to me—I dreaded the prospect of meditation. But the more I didn't want to think about meditation, the more I thought about it. Ean was also encouraging me to try it. We'd often begin our sessions with some deep breathing. Breathing, he told me, was an important tool in meditation. It was easy enough to "focus on my breath" when he was guiding me to do it, but the thought of doing it on my own was daunting.

It was *The One You Feed* podcast that finally gave me a much-needed push. An interviewee mentioned someone named Pema Chodron. Both the interviewer and the interviewee talked about how much they loved her and one of them said something like, "I don't know what I'd do without her." After the podcast was over, I searched for Pema Chodron. But when I saw her picture, a nun with a shaved head, I was disappointed. I wasn't excited about reading something written by a nun—it might be full of religious stuff—and that made me uncomfortable. But more research showed me that Chodron is an extremely popular writer on meditation and that she writes for a secular audience. As I scanned through her titles on the Internet, my eye landed on one called *How to Meditate*. But it wasn't the title that caught my attention, it was the sub-title, *A Practical Guide to Making Friends with Your Mind*.

Friends? With my mind? The idea brought back the letter I had written when I first embarked on this project. The most difficult thing about writing it were those three closing words, I love you. As my mouse hovered over the buy button, it struck me that the idea of learning how to make friends with myself might be valuable, and Chodron was offering me a guide on how to do that through meditation. I bought the book. It was time to do this meditation thing.

Through Chodron's book and others, I learned that it's important to have a few things in place for regular meditation practice. One was a quiet, private space to meditate in. Given that there were only two people in my household, this was easy enough. There was a little alcove beside our kitchen and I decided that this would be my space. Second, I needed to choose a time of day to stick to. I decided I would try out a few different times and decide later. Finally, I needed to choose how long I was going to meditate for. Chodron suggests twenty minutes for beginners, but that seemed insane. I decided to start with ten.

On day one I put a sofa cushion on the floor and sat down, cross-legged and straight-backed, even though all the books say you can sit in whatever position is comfortable for you, whether that's on a chair, a meditation bench, or lying down if you can keep yourself awake. I set the timer on my phone for ten minutes, placed my hands on my knees, and shut my eyes. Now meditate, I commanded.

Chodron encourages meditators to pay attention to the breath, which puts us into a more relaxed state, thereby helping to soothe and stabilize our busy minds. Like Ean had taught me, I breathed deeply, in and out. My brain was instantly flooded with thoughts: What if Chris comes home early and sees me doing this? I would be so embarrassed. I'm hungry, what am I going to make for dinner? I gotta get that report edited tonight. Shit, why didn't I do it earlier? What am I going to do for a workout tomorrow, swim, or climb, or yoga? Maybe go for a hike, weather should be good. If it's not, I could do yoga instead. I could make pasta for dinner. No, eat a salad. But I don't want a salad. Was that a key in the lock? Is Chris home?

And it was so noisy! Why was every neighbour on my block using their weed whacker? I squeezed my eyes tighter and thought I'll never be able to meditate with all this noise. I need to choose a much quieter place. Like the bathroom. Would the bathroom work? That would be weird. I don't want salad. Oh, there's some leftover rice I could eat. I could mix that with the salad. Oh my God, how much longer?

I opened my eyes to check my phone but not even two minutes had passed. I still had eight minutes to go. This was horrible! I knew I wouldn't be able to do it. Right, focus on my breath. I listened to my inhale and then listened to my exhale. What if I forget to breathe? What if I suffocate? Can I die meditating? Has anyone died meditating? OK, focus on your breath. I remembered someone likening the inflow and outflow of breath to opening and closing a door, so I held that image in my mind and kept trying to breathe slowly.

A flurry of thoughts immediately popped up again. My irritation rose at the noise outside my window. I wanted to scream at the people across the street, Shut the fuck up! Don't you know I'm meditating? I was angry, my shoulders were tense, and I was wasting time thinking stupid, useless thoughts. I hated this so much. The timer went off at what felt like an hour later. Making friends with my mind! Ha! Never.

Ean assured me that my experience was perfectly natural. The thoughts would always be there, he explained. I couldn't turn them off but I could detach myself from them so I could observe them. Like Tolle said, I could watch the thinker. Ean used a train analogy to help me understand. Imagine each thought as a boxcar on a train. Thoughts, like boxcars, would come along, pass, then another one would come along, pass, then another one. He encouraged me to see the thought—the boxcar—acknowledge it, and then let it pass. The next one would come along soon enough. Eventually, he said, I might get to the point where I became aware of the space between the boxcars, that is, the space between the thoughts, or the "gap," as Tolle called it, and I would experience who I was beyond this jumble of incessant thinking.

A week later I tried again. This time, I had trains on the brain. Just think of your thoughts as boxcars, I told myself. But the boxcars came quickly, too quickly. Thoughts on top of thoughts came in, like double-decker boxcars. My thoughts felt more akin to a Japanese bullet train and when the ten minutes was up, I felt like I had been hit by one.

I complained to Ean that his analogy didn't work, and that I was so confused by the train idea that I had forgotten to focus on my breath. He asked me to describe the train I'd experienced. The phrase that immediately came to mind was a runaway train. "Congratulations," Ean said. "You're seeing your thoughts for what they are. A runaway train. You are becoming aware of how your thoughts operate."

Seeing my thoughts in action was the point of meditation. It didn't matter what the thoughts were. The purpose was to see the amount of thoughts, how quickly they passed by, and how quickly others took their place. In daily life, Ean explained, we tend to jump on a boxcar-thought and go for a ride. Thoughts take us out of the present moment and into the past or future. How many boxcars had I ridden all the way to the "worst case scenario" station? Meditation teaches us how to recognize that we have jumped on a car but, also, how we can choose to jump off, come back to the present, and regain that state of mind that brings clarity, insight, joy, and peace. I was reminded of the moment with my cellphone in my car. My hand hovering over the passenger seat, I saw that I had not impulsively acted on the urge to pick it up—I had let that boxcar go by. The outcome of that single action was a significant decrease in the odds of a future car accident.

Intellectually, this all made sense to me but it didn't get any easier over the next few weeks. I would dread sitting down for those ten minutes and when I did my thoughts would again feel like a freight train barrelling down on me. Eventually, sometimes I was able to recognize when I had jumped onto a boxcar and gone for a ride by following a thought that took me into a memory, planning, worrying, or a daydream. Noticing I was caught up in thinking would take me anywhere from thirty seconds to the entire ten-minute meditation session. Each time I noticed, I would internally sigh in frustration and come back to my breath, only to be swept up again and again. Similar to when I was learning to ski, I wondered the same thing about meditation: When did this get enjoyable? When did these so-called wonderful feelings of peace and bliss start? I knew that it was going to take a lot of practice, like skiing, but *not* dreading meditation seemed like a long, long way away.

One morning in August, I was waiting to catch the SeaBus, a fifteen-minute ferry that would take me to downtown Vancouver for a meeting. Normally, I would check my phone or read a book while I waited for the SeaBus to pull in. This day, though, I decided to read the public notices and posters tacked up on the station wall. Right away one poster leapt out:

DISCOVER MINDFULNESS-AWARENESS MEDITATION

FREE DROP-IN MEDITATION

EVERY MONDAY, 7PM–8PM

Most of the books I was reading encouraged joining a meditation group. Here was one just a few streets away from my house, held at a time that was perfectly feasible for me. I didn't like that it was held in a church, and the fact that it was an hour long seemed particularly daunting, but I wasn't having a lot of success on my own. Maybe a group would help.

A few weeks later I showed up on a Monday evening. I hadn't been in a church in over a decade and so I felt awkward walking up the front steps. A sign on the door pointed the way to the meditation group and there was a donation box explaining that any money collected would go to the rental of the church.

I was surprised to see about thirty-five people there. Most sat in pews, but as I made my way up farther into the church, I noticed cushions for people to sit on. I was used to sitting on the floor, so I grabbed one. Looking around, I expected to see a bunch of sad-looking people desperate to feel better but everyone looked normal and many were chatting happily with each other. The group included as many men as women (surprising to me) and the age range appeared to run from people in their mid-twenties to those in their seventies and possibly eighties.

The instructor, Jennifer, sat on a chair at the front of the church holding a smartphone. At seven o'clock she said, "Welcome everyone, thank you for coming. Is there anyone here for the first time?" I put up my hand and looked around the room. Other hands showed me I was by no means the only first timer. Jennifer then asked, "Is this the first time meditating for anyone?" Again, a few hands. But not mine. That helped me relax a little more. I wasn't completely out of my element. I had assumed that we would have to sit still for a full hour, but Jennifer explained that we would only sit for twenty minutes and then do a walking meditation and then sit for another twenty minutes. I was relieved, but even though the hour was broken up, this would still be the longest meditation I would have ever done. Jennifer instructed us to focus on our breath. If we got carried away by our thoughts, she said, just come back to the breath. She set the timer on her phone for twenty minutes and we began.

Immediately I was aware of people breathing around me, then the traffic outside the windows, the noises made by the water pipes in the church, and people shifting in their seats. But for the most part, the room was quiet and I was aware of being among people doing the exact same thing I was. It was soothing: there was nothing else I could do, nowhere else I could go, so I sat there and focused on my breath. Inhale, exhale. Inhale, exhale. The thoughts quickly came and I jumped on some and watched others go. Because I knew there were a few people who had never meditated before, I had an idea what they might be experiencing and this made me feel more confident. Hello, achiever. The twenty minutes went by faster than I thought it would.

Next, we would do a walking meditation. The point of this, Jennifer explained, was to focus on the feeling of our feet on the floor, nothing else. She demonstrated how to fold our hands in front of our stomach so they wouldn't be distracting and thus help heighten our awareness of walking. We would walk, single file, twice around the inside perimeter of the church. The first lap felt totally weird. Was I walking too fast? Too slow? Should I look up or down? Were people looking at me? But halfway through the second lap, I felt something akin to what I had felt when I was chopping vegetables in my kitchen a few weeks ago. A sense of peace came over me. I could feel the soles of my feet against the carpet, and the more I focused on the sensation, the stronger this sense of peace got. I felt like I could walk for hours. Tears prickled my eyes. I was deeply calm, happy, and present, and all I was doing was walking. Too quickly it was over, and it was back to our spots for the next twenty minutes. I sat down on my cushion, shut my eyes, and relived the feeling of walking. I commended myself for getting it right. Then I fell asleep.

A few minutes later, I woke with a start. Had anyone seen me? Had I snored? Falling asleep meditating on my own was not uncommon, but I was mortified that I had done it in front of other people. I chastised myself for a few minutes. What was the point of coming if I was just going to sleep through it? Eventually, I forced myself to re-focus on my breath and I calmed down. By the end of the session, I felt peaceful and relaxed. I had done it. Gotten through the hour. But I had also gotten from the hour. There was no denying that having other people around was motivating. And, there was no denying that I had experienced something I wanted more of during the walking meditation. I would go back.

My experience the following Monday was entirely different. I was irritated from the moment I sat down to the moment the hour ended. Someone was snoring, though at least it wasn't me. The person behind me kept fidgeting. The traffic seemed especially bad and I wanted to scream at the kids playing outside. Even the walking meditation was terrible. I kept waiting for the same feeling of presence to happen again. I willed the feeling to come. Come on already. Feel good. Nothing. I went home dejected.

I had a feeling that what I had experienced the first week of the group meditation was something my books referred to as "beginner's mind." By not knowing what to expect, everything was new which meant anything was possible—I had not limited myself with expectations. I had experienced this with climbing. As a beginner, with no expectations, I had loved climbing and was able to enjoy the sheer pleasure of it. As I became more skilled, I expected to continually improve and brought those expectations to each workout. The more expectations I brought, the less I enjoyed climbing. If my expectations weren't met, I would feel like the session was wasted.

It was the same with the first week of group meditation. The walking meditation was totally new to me—I had a clear, open-to-everything, beginner's mind. And something happened that felt good. But the following week, I brought an expectation of having the same feeling into the walking meditation. And the feeling didn't happen. It was a valuable lesson. What I needed to do was approach *every* meditation session with a beginner's mind. Expect nothing. Replace expectation with curiosity.

As I continued to meditate on my own at home, I became aware of expectations creeping into my thoughts. Sometimes I had enough presence to see these expectations, acknowledge them, and return to focusing on my breath. I practiced this repeatedly, dozens of times a session. Cultivating a beginner's mind is especially difficult for strivers who prefer a sense of progression and success. I was learning that wanting to be good at meditation defeats the purpose of meditation. I was also beginning to understand that meditation was showing me that the concept of striving evaporates when one is experiencing the present moment. Meditation was also proof of the value of curiosity. I felt a tug of appreciation for myself because curiosity was something of which I had deep reserves.

◆

SINCE I HAD seen the group meditation poster on the wall at the SeaBus terminal, I started keeping watch to see what else was posted. One day I saw a sign for a one-day meditation retreat. Many of the authors I was reading talked about going on retreats, essentially extended periods of meditation. This non-denominational retreat would also be held in a church and was described as a day of contemplation, interspersed with occasional readings of text and poems. I loved that word, contemplation. It seemed much softer than thinking and, between all my reading and my meditation, I had loads of stuff to contemplate. Plus, a day with no books seemed like an interesting challenge. I had concerns about boredom and a potentially wasted summer Saturday, but I found myself registering anyway. As I put the phone down, I realized that I would have never done anything like this six months ago.

On the morning of the retreat, I got up early, ate breakfast, put on comfortable clothes, and checked in at the church. There were about twenty-five of us. This time, I was one of the younger participants. Chairs were placed in a circle at the altar and we each took one, all in silence. The first hour or so was a mixture of the retreat leaders reading a poem or a piece of writing, and then we would sit and contemplate what we had heard. After, a short piece of music, a jazz arrangement, was played, then more contemplation. The contemplation sessions were short and I enjoyed them. I was full of thoughts, but some of them did pertain to the piece of writing or music. Then, we were told we would sit in silence for an hour. I had a feeling something like this would be part of the day, but an hour? With nothing to do?

Other people got up to find pews to sit on, but before doing so myself, I went to the refreshments table and made myself some herbal tea. I took the mug back to a pew and curled up against the wood. I cupped my hands around the mug and took a sip. I felt my palms against the porcelain and experienced the warmth of the tea. I took another sip and again felt the mug in my hands. I felt the pew underneath me, and then I felt a warmth come over me. I realized I was completely at peace. I didn't want to move. I didn't want to talk. I didn't want to do anything except experience more of what I was experiencing right at that moment.

A few weeks earlier I'd read somewhere that happiness is wanting what you have. In that moment, my hands cupping the mug of tea, I understood that phrase. I wanted nothing more than that cup of tea in the silence of the church. I contemplated something that I had read in Tolle's book. He said we are always in "The Now." The past is gone and the future hasn't happened. It is always now, it can only be now. We can only experience one moment at a time. While we may yearn for a future when we will be happy, or worry about what will happen next, or relive what just happened, the only thing ever happening is life right now. In this instant. And then that instant is gone and replaced with a new instant. What a wonderful way to live one's life, I thought, experiencing each moment fully as it happens. A few months earlier, I'd had the idea that one could find happiness *on the way* to achievements. In the church that day, it occurred to me that maybe I didn't need achievements at all.

Two other interesting things happened during that retreat. First, lunch was eaten silently and alone. I'd never eaten a meal on my own where I didn't have something to read or something to watch on TV to distract me. A cup of tea was one thing, but eating an entire meal with no other stimulation made me feel slightly panicky. At least, that was my expectation as I chose my sandwich and cookies. All I had to focus on was the food. I had thirty minutes with nothing to do but eat.

I took a bite and chewed slowly. I tasted the bread and the mustard and the cheese. I felt the texture of each ingredient. I swallowed and looked at my sandwich. I looked at the colours, the flecks of wheat in the bread. I took another small bite and chewed slowly. The taste was stronger this time; I could taste the sourness and then the heat of the mustard. I could taste the creaminess and the saltiness of the cheese. The slower I ate, the more delicious the sandwich became. I did the same with a couple of cookies and enjoyed the different tastes and textures as well. If I felt my mind wandering, I would take another bite of cookie and focus on what my mouth was doing, what my tongue was tasting. I was meditating but meditating while doing something.

This had to be that thing I was reading about: mindfulness. Being with whatever you are doing one hundred percent and using the experience to stay present. If the mind wanders, keep coming back to the task and focus. Fill your mind with what you are doing and clear out the distractions. I saw that having a task, such as eating, was a great way to apply my mind so that it didn't run away on me. The task quieted the left-brain interpreter. I was feeling the same way as I did when I drank my cup of tea. Peaceful and calm. Full. Present. Happy.

After lunch, we were encouraged to go for a solo half-hour walk in the neighbourhood surrounding the church in another exercise of mindfulness. I couldn't remember a time I had gone for a walk on my own without a purpose or a destination. My habitual expectation of boredom flared up, and again I worked to set it aside in favour of curiosity, even if I had a nagging feeling that this was going to be a painful experience. No one to talk to, nowhere to go. Just stroll. And it was painful for the first fifteen minutes or so. I was concerned about what people on their front lawns might think watching me walk around aimlessly. I tried to focus on the feeling of the sidewalk beneath my feet but was quickly distracted by noticing that I was feeling bored and uncomfortable. Normally, I had my phone in my hand when I walked, often texting or listening to music. With no phone, I barely knew what to do with my hands. I became aware of my arms swinging at my sides. With nothing to do, the houses and trees became my stimuli. My eyes darted around to plants, hedges, colourful doors, kids' bicycles, and a cat. I stopped and watched it move through a front yard toward me and I stooped down to pet it—my only interaction with another being so far that day. I felt the softness of the cat's fur and my mood shifted.

I continued my walk looking at things more slowly now, resting my eyes for a few seconds, as opposed to trying to take in everything. Again, a feeling of peace washed over me. I was enjoying this. But it was soon back to the church for the rest of the afternoon for more poems and music. As the retreat came to a close, I was extremely aware of not wanting to talk to anyone. Being silent was freeing and I didn't want it to end. Even after a full day of silence, I wasn't craving conversation, my content couch, food, or wine. I wasn't craving anything.

There was some group work at the end of the day where the facilitator had us pair up and discuss our reactions to the retreat. The feeling of peace seemed common to many of us. Like me, a few people also acknowledged they were reticent to break the silence. The facilitator told us that these types of retreats allowed us to remember what it felt like to be present and when we could contemplate rather than randomly think. We were encouraged to take this mindfulness back into our daily lives. As I drove home, I made a list of the things I wanted to change. I wanted to eat my meals slowly and mindfully. I wanted to go for walks with no destination.

Oh, beginner's mind. Of course, the retreat had been powerful for me because I was experiencing many of these things for the first time. Taking this back to daily life was a different story. The next day, I tried to eat my breakfast without reading the paper. But reading while eating was a twenty-year-old habit, and I had no success that morning or subsequent mornings in breaking it. And I didn't go for any aimless, meandering walks. I continued to text as I crossed the street. I was starting to understand what the retreat facilitator meant when he described these retreats as "reminders." It was so easy to forget the things that made us peaceful when daily life swallowed us up.

Meanwhile, I continued to practice my meditation. Not every day, I'd skip a few days and then feel guilty and sit down for a short session. Excuses were easy to find to avoid it. I'd tell myself I was too hungry to meditate, or that I hadn't slept enough and needed ten more minutes in bed, or that I had to watch one more episode of whatever show I was into. But when I did sit down, my session almost always taught me something. Meditation was experiential learning—I was my best teacher. Meditation showed me how fast my mind was spitting out thoughts, or when I was irritated, judging myself, or setting expectations, or when I was stuck on something that had happened in the past. It showed me how much I ruminated and worried.

My books on meditation told me that we are not our thoughts. How could we be if we can separate ourselves from our thoughts to watch them? But the practice of meditation was allowing me to experience the truth of that statement. The very moment I became aware that I had jumped on a boxcar, I had a choice to jump off. The thoughts kept flowing right on by, independent of me watching them. I recognized that my achiever fever was the Orient Express.

One of my favourite metaphors for meditation is seeing our thoughts as a waterfall. The waterfall will never dry up because our thoughts will never stop—they continue to pour over the cliff. When I meditate, my job is to imagine myself beside a waterfall and watch the stream of my thoughts as they descend. It is this metaphor that I think about when I recall the phrase, I wish I could get out of my own way. My assumption was that I had to bulldoze through something to do that. But all I needed to do was sit beside a waterfall and watch.

And I think that's what making friends with our mind means. Seeing the waterfall for the spectacularly creative force that it is but remembering that we don't have to go over the edge with it. Meditation was helping me to look out for myself by reminding me I had a choice to follow a negative thought or not. As I became more diligent in practicing mediation, I saw two other companions looking out for me as well—someone called determination and the other named discipline. Realizing that it would take the achiever within me to help dissipate my fever made me laugh.

Chapter 7

A DIFFERENT KIND
OF GROWTH

I TRAVEL A lot for work, whether it be for moderating focus groups, pitching new business, or visiting clients. Wherever I go, I am diligent about finding a place to work out because more than four days without exercise makes me feel tired and sluggish. Eight months into my work with Ean, I was finding the same with my inner workout. Four-plus days with no meditation made me feel antsy. Understanding the importance of attending to my inner self on a regular basis, I began to look for drop-in meditation groups on the road. Some were way too strange for me, like the one in San Diego where we chanted and sang along to a harmonium for an hour. Well, the group did. I just waited for it to be over. And some were exactly what I needed.

My favourite meditation drop-in took place in San Francisco. It was located a few streets behind the head office of a major tech company, and I loved the idea of its scraggly prayer flags juxtaposed against the enormous building. In the session I attended, we meditated for an hour (still a long time for me at that point) and then had a group discussion. In the discussion, we were asked to talk about something that was bothering us. I brought up my business and explained that while we had been growing steadily over the last six years, revenue appeared to be stalling. Though I believed I had the right mix of people and some strong, repeat clients, the currently slow quarter was making me anxious. I had recently snapped at a co-worker, for example, and was preoccupied with "what if" scenarios. There were a couple of other business owners in the group and one of them raised her hand. What she said, as best I could recall later that evening in my journal, was something like this

I treat my company as a living, breathing animal. It's alive, like us humans. Just like we breathe, expanding and contracting, so too does my business. And, because my business is alive, it can also be a hot mess. If I drew it on paper right now, it would just be a big scribble. Rather than concentrating on growth, I try to remain aware of how I am treating this living, breathing being. When it acts up, when it doesn't do what I want it to, can I still love it? My business offers me a constant opportunity to learn about myself and the more I learn, the more we both grow.

I thought about that woman's words for weeks. Never had I thought of my business as a living being, something that could both expand and contract. Rather, my business was something that needed to expand, and if it wasn't growing, if it wasn't moving in the right direction, something was wrong. I obviously hadn't planned well enough or worried the right worries. Thinking of it as a living being, as something that had a life of its own outside of my control, was intriguing. And, when I stopped to think about it, I saw that my business had indeed expanded and contracted over the years—some quarters were great, some less so. New employees joined, others moved on. Some organizations became regular clients, others were one-offs. It was a living being. What could I do to stop my business from cowering every time I shook my finger at it? How could I treat it better? This woman had given me the idea that I could learn to love my business. I could learn to love the highs and the lows and even celebrate the occasional hot mess. There is something delightful in that phrase, hot mess, because it has a sense of humour. What if I could bring that sense of humour to my business? And, more importantly, as the woman had said, recognize that those hot messes represented opportunities for growth.

✦

I WAS NOW two thirds of the way through my year with Ean. My co-workers told me that I seemed different, calmer, more relaxed, quicker to laugh. One of my sisters told me that I seemed more grounded. The other told me she was worried that I had lost my spark because I was quieter. I brooded on this for a few days and realized that I was quieter because I was learning to listen. I was less likely to think ahead to the next funny story, or the next "impressive" piece of information to share, and more likely to pay attention to what was going on around me. I was also feeling lighter—both physically (I had lost a few pounds by

this point working with Ean) and mentally. The Judge was quieter and I was sleeping soundly.

I was also aware that it had been a desire for personal growth
and self-improvement that led to this mesearch project, thanks
to my achiever fever. But rather than blame the fever, I was
beginning to see how useful it had been for putting me on this
path in the first place. Could I love my achiever fever, just like
the woman in the meditation group learned to love her business? It was my suffering that had led to my now daily sense of
curiosity, peacefulness, and, occasionally, joy. It was my desire
to speed up that had led me to learn how to slow down. There
was something about this mesearch process that felt much more
sustainable than propelling myself along with the occasional
boosts of happiness I used to get from reaching my goals. Either
way, though, I still had a deep desire for growth.

A few months earlier, Ean had me read about the "Six Human
Needs" as put forth by psychologist Cloé Madanes and popu-
larized by Tony Robbins. These six needs are certainty, variety,
significance, love/connection, growth, and contribution. All of
us have these needs in some way, shape, or form, but often one
pulls at us more powerfully than the others. When Ean asked
which one was most meaningful to me, only one word leapt
out—growth. Professional growth. Financial growth. Intellec-
tual growth. Growth in my sport activities. Growth in my relationships. Grow, lead, improve, build, progress, achieve! This
was my modus operandi.

This need for forward momentum had been my engine for as
long as I could remember, as it was for many of the achievers I
surveyed. One of the survey questions asked the respondents to
fill in the blank to the statement, "If I am not achieving, I am...."
Many used words and phrases like failing, worthless, stagnant,

stuck, standing still, going backward and, perhaps most discon-
certing, dying. The problem with this focus on growth, however, is that it led to a corresponding growth in my achiever
fever. My obsession with growth led to a festering sense of
absence in my life, but I wasn't quite sure what was missing. In
fact, almost thirty percent of the surveyed achievers say they
feel something in their life is missing, but they don't know what
it is.

The first clue that I might want to question my concept of
growth came from a book on meditation. Jon Kabat-Zinn is a
professor emeritus of medicine at the University of Massachusetts
Medical School. He approaches meditation from a science-based
background and was responsible for starting a stress reduction
program called MBSR—mindfulness-based stress reduction. The
program is now offered all over the world, in universities, jails,
and medical institutions, and Kabat-Zinn is considered one of
the foremost experts on meditation and mindfulness. It was the
following passage in Kabat-Zinn's book that struck me: "Ordi-
narily, when we undertake something, it is only natural to expect
a desirable outcome for our efforts. We want to see results, even
if it is only a pleasant feeling. The sole exception I can think of is
meditation. Meditation is the only intentional, systematic human
activity which at bottom is about *not* trying to improve yourself
or get anywhere else, but simply to realize where you already
are.... It would not quite be accurate to call meditation a 'doing.'
It is more accurately described as a 'being.'"[20]

The first time I read this I thought what the hell is the point
of meditation if it's not going to improve me? But the line
also resonated with me for a deeper, unknown reason. When
I mentioned this to Ean, he handed me a pencil and paper
and asked me to draw what I thought growth looked like. I

knew enough by now to understand that there were peaks and valleys in any growth chart. So I tried to show him how sophisticated I was by drawing a zigzag line from the bottom left corner to the top right. My picture resembled a flourishing stock index: small dips but successively larger climbs. "You have to have some valleys to have the peaks," I sagely explained to him.

Ean then took the pencil from me and turned the page over. "Let me show you a different way to think about growth," he said. He drew a wide horizontal oval at the bottom of the page and then kept the pencil spiralling around in horizontal loops. As he drew, he gradually moved his pencil upwards and the loops got smaller and smaller until he stopped drawing. I looked at him not knowing where he was going with this.

"Think about this as a three-dimensional image," he said. I looked again. Now his drawing resembled an upside-down tornado or a coiled snake. Ean put the pencil point at the tip of what would be the snake's tail. "This is you born," he said. "As a baby, you know nothing about surviving in the world and you are totally dependent on your parents for knowledge. You are in someone else's care entirely and this is when the circle is the widest. But as you get older, and become more independent, that knowledge is coming more from you now, so the circle becomes a little narrower. As you age, you continue going around in circles, feeling like you are often in the same place over and over again. You want to progress, but you keep encountering the same problems. This is why the spirals don't seem to be going anywhere."

I could relate to this. Even though my life did appear to be moving forward, I often felt like I kept coming back to these feelings of self-doubt and fear. Going around in circles was an apt description. So I asked Ean, "What happens to make the spirals get narrower eventually?"

"You may think you are going around in circles," he replied, "but you are a different person every step you take along the circle. You are constantly impacted by what is going on around you, by who you encounter, by the experiences you have. You are constantly changing. Eventually, you will notice patterns to your experiences. Which is exactly what you've done. You started this project because you became aware of a pattern. As you become more aware of these patterns, you learn more and more about yourself so that you become more closely connected to your centre. You start to live your life based on who you really are rather than basing it on external validation. The spirals continue to narrow as you continue to find your centre. This is another way to look at growth."

I stared at the diagram. In my world, growth was obvious and could be measured in things like revenue, profit, climbing grades, and swim times. What Ean was saying was something completely different. Growth was subtler, not the full-steam ahead, fist raised in the air striving that I was used to.

Ean had talked about "my centre" before; he'd even written it into the original objectives of our project contract: "Claire will learn to centre herself." And here it was again in this growth diagram. Ean told me that as I was learning who I was, I was becoming more connected with myself. This, Ean said, is inner growth. This is where true confidence comes from, when what you do and say is aligned with who you really are, not what you think you should be.

I was quiet because I knew intuitively he was right. The more I listened to myself, the more connected and grounded I felt, and the more my achiever fever would dissipate. Growth did not have to be something external, something that could be measured by other people; growth could be internal. In fact, Ean explained, the more centred I became, the more powerful I would be. Not a "take over the world" sort of power, but rather a quiet confidence that I could do whatever I wanted to do.

Later that evening, as I thought about Ean's explanation of going around in circles, I realized that, in this model, there was no way to go backwards because, even though it may not feel like it, I was constantly learning. Sometimes it took a hot mess to see the patterns, and that seeing, that awareness, could be transformative. I just had to welcome the hot messes.

✦

MY COMMUTES TO Kung Fu practice were the perfect time to listen to podcasts. Snarled in traffic after a busy day, longing to be lounging at home, I was often in a lousy mood, and *The One You Feed* podcasts usually helped to make the car ride a little more enjoyable. One afternoon the podcast host, Eric Zimmer, interviewed Carol Dweck, the author of a book called *Mindset: The New Psychology of Success.* I was so captivated by her description of "fixed" and "growth" mindsets, I had to pull over and take notes.

Dweck explains that our "mindset" is based on the beliefs we hold about ourselves and that these mindsets will drive not just our decision-making but also how we feel about ourselves. Her a-ha moment came during her early research days when she was observing children trying to solve difficult puzzles. As she expected, most of them couldn't figure out the puzzles and were frustrated. But there were a couple of kids who reacted in a different way. Though the solution wasn't coming to these kids any faster than it was for the others, these other kids talked about enjoying the challenge. Dweck was shocked when she realized these kids embraced the failure of their attempts at the puzzle. What did these kids know that she didn't? This was the beginning of her research into mindset.

Most of us, according to Dweck, believe that we have an aptitude for certain things and not for others and that we see this aptitude as "fixed" or "innate." We know what we're good at because failure shows us what we're bad at. Her research showed that this belief is not "law" but rather indicative of having a "fixed mindset." Those of us with a fixed mindset, she notes, tend to feel an urgency to prove that we are good at certain things because we are aware we are not good at others.[21]

That "urgency to prove" had been with me forever. I thought back to my school days where I was a good student in English and a poor one in math. Rather than spending additional time on math, I devoted my time to English because I needed to be seen as a top student. This set in motion a fixed mindset around numbers, and I believed I had no aptitude for math. To this day, I am convinced that it was calculus in grade twelve that gave me mono. No wonder I struggled with understanding my finances—I had set up a thick mental barrier.

And there were other areas where I could now identify a fixed mindset: my belief that I can't learn a new language, feeling helpless when my technology doesn't work (I once threw a computer mouse at the wall so hard it exploded), assuming I am terrible with directions, my acceptance that I cannot draw or understand how a car works. When presented with a task in any of these categories, my fixed mindset kicks in and limits the effort I make. Because I believe that I am tackling something that I am not "built for," I sense failure before I even try, which usually means I don't. When I do work up the courage to try something that I believe I am innately bad at, mountain biking for example, and something goes wrong, I use it as proof that I wasn't meant to be a mountain biker.

When Chris and I were travelling around the world, we did a lot of mountain biking and I was beginning to enjoy it. On my thirty-fifth birthday, Chris took me down a more advanced route. Within a few minutes, I was out of control. My fixed mindset kicked in—you don't know what you're doing, this is not your thing—and rather than try and right myself and remember my technique, I gave in to fear and fell over my handlebars. All I got was a broken finger, but as far as I was concerned, it was a sign that I wasn't cut out to be a mountain biker. There is comfort in believing one is right.

A growth mindset, on the other hand, is a totally different animal. Dweck explains this mindset as a belief "that your basic qualities are things you can cultivate through your efforts.... The passion for stretching yourself and sticking to it, even (or especially) when it's not going well, is the hallmark of the growth mindset. This is the mindset that allows people to thrive during some of the most challenging times in their lives."[22]

The kids in Dweck's experiment who embraced failure had a growth mindset—they thrived on not getting it right. To a person with a growth mindset, failure is an opportunity to learn and improve, whereas failure to a fixed mindset person is proof that they were right about themselves and a signal to stop trying. This concept of a growth mindset makes me remember something my dad used to say—"I went to the school of hard knocks." He'd often say it in response to something I was complaining about such as not doing well on a test, or having a fight with a friend. It drove me nuts because I wanted him to tell me not to worry and that everything was going to be OK. Now I could see that people with a growth mindset relish a "hard knock" every so often. As Ean often said, there was always a gift to be found in everything that went wrong. If I could see my trials and tribulations as gifts, I could foster my own growth mindset.

It was easy to practice this at work because, as a project-based business, there are so many occasions for obstacles. If an employee complained that something had gone wrong, I could always find something about the snafu that would help them learn something. I would tell them that the "hard knock" was an opportunity to think creatively. I would then watch as they tried different approaches to bring the project back on track. When the project ended successfully, I could see that the employee had gained much more from the experience than they would have had the project gone according to the original plan. Not only had they had an opportunity to take a risk and try something new, they gained confidence as they watched their decision play out successfully, and I watched them jubilantly tell their co-workers about what they had learned. They thrived through the process whereas, it occurred to me, someone with a fixed mindset strived. I also realized that language was indicative of someone's mindset, and I started to pay more attention when I heard myself, co-workers, friends, and family say things like: "I'm terrible at that," "I always screw that up," "I'm never going to be able to...." It was almost comical how often we said it, but frightening when I thought back to Dweck's words, "the view you adopt for yourself profoundly affects the way you lead your life."[23]

I had the perfect opportunity to see an example of someone with a growth mindset a few days later in one of my peer group sessions with L3. As I have already described, I spent many hours in L3 thinking I was an imposter and that I couldn't possibly be adding value to the group. I'd feel my stomach clench and grit my teeth as we discussed topics that I had no experience in. My self-doubt would completely deflate me and, at the end of many sessions, I was resigned to dropping out. But I didn't. Even with all the emotional and even physical discomfort, I kept going back. Even with my self-doubt and imposter syndrome, I kept showing up. I was building confidence and competence in a way I hadn't understood. And I realized I went back not out of loyalty but because, unbeknownst to me, I had a growth mindset.

Later, when explaining my insight to Ean, he honed in on my description of physical discomfort in L3 sessions. The discomfort or pain, he explained, is the cue that there is something to learn about yourself. If you pay attention, he said, you cannot help but grow. The body is often the best teacher when it comes to growth. But you need the awareness to notice your physical state, the desire to pay attention to it, the patience to name it, and then the discipline to look at it. I still have difficulty with this process. It's so much easier to make a martini.

Over the last eight months, anytime I had mentioned feeling stressed, Ean would ask me where I felt it in my body. At first, I had difficulty identifying a physical response to my emotional discomfort. Despite being a swimmer and a climber, I had no strong mind/body connection. I couldn't tell the difference between which pain was the product of a hard workout, a missed meal, feeling tired, or an injury, and which pain was stress-related. But, over time, I began to recognize how my body reacted to stress. I began to understand the difference between mechanical pain, like pain caused by an injury or overexertion, and the emotional pain caused by anxiety, fear, or worry.

As Ean and I continued to talk about physical reactions to stress, I started to become more aware of my stomach clenching in fear if I thought I was about to receive bad news, my jaw tightening if I was in a precarious situation in traffic, or my toes curling if I was angry. Once I could feel and describe these physical sensations, Ean asked me to locate the place of physical pressure and imagine it as a shape. The image that would often float up was of a steel plate in my upper back. Ean would then ask me which emotion the plate represented. An emotion would always bubble up: anger, sadness, nervousness, frustration, worry. Ean would then ask me if there was a deeper emotion powering it and the answer was almost always the same—fear.

Fear of being a bad boss
Fear of my employees leaving
Fear of my clients leaving
Fear of my business failing
Fear that I wasn't trying hard enough
Fear that I wasn't living up to my potential
Fear that my family was angry with me
Fear that I hadn't accomplished what I should have by now
Fear that I was making the wrong decision
Fear that I would always feel like this

Visualizing helped to make the emotion more tangible and helped me verbalize what I was feeling. Ean was trying to show me that these physical feelings—the tightness, numbness, and constricted breathing—were my body telling me to pay attention. My body was waving a red flag saying, "Hey! Look at this! Investigate this!" But acknowledging the red flag meant I would have to engage that discomfort. Like most human beings, when

I am not comfortable, I want to get comfortable. In hindsight, I see how much time I've spent distracting myself because I would rather the discomfort just go away.

Some of my favourite distractions are my phone, food, alcohol, TV, reading, and sleep. On the surface these activities appear like things any normal person would do in the process of relaxation, but it's the intention behind them that makes them either relaxing or stress-avoidance distractions. The trick is identifying when these distractions have morphed from enjoying some simple down time to self-sabotaging behaviours. The latter can lead to problems such as overeating or drinking. Sixty percent of the achievers I surveyed say they use food more often than they'd like to feel better, and fifty percent use alcohol to avoid stress-related emotions. When these activities are automatic reactions rather than conscious and informed choices, that's when they are more of a distraction than a complement to a full life. And that's when we hamper our growth.

✦

ONE NIGHT, I was out with a large group of friends, a scenario that often makes me anxious. I sat down, ordered a drink, and almost immediately became aware of my chest tightening. The conversation was about bikes and I didn't have anything to add to it. My chest got tighter. The thought crossed my mind that I wanted another drink and I understood that the tension in my chest was fear. What was I scared of? I let my mind go blank and there it was: fear of being perceived as boring.

Over the next ten minutes, I watched myself trying to change the conversation to a topic I was more familiar with. When that didn't work, I watched the fear turn to frustration. My toes were clenching, a sure sign of anger. I watched myself take seconds and then thirds of a rice dish to comfort myself. Obviously, this fear of being boring was something that needed to be looked at more closely later. But for the moment, I was starting to enjoy watching my reactions, which meant I was present, and before I knew it, I was smiling and naturally engaging in the conversation. I hadn't negated any of my thoughts by distracting myself from them, but nor did I hold onto them for longer than a few minutes. I was present, I was aware, I was observing. In a way, I was meditating, but among other people. I had turned an uncomfortable situation into an interesting, insightful one by being curious rather than trying to distract myself from my feelings.

Today, I'm much more aware of my physical reactions to feelings of fear, anxiety, or worry. But my body also lets me know what happens when I am centred. If I'm walking, I can feel the soles of my feet. If I'm sitting, I can feel the top of my chest expanding. If I'm standing, I feel a quiet energy deep in my stomach. I feel grounded, with no desire to go anywhere or do anything, and it is in this state that I do much more than grow. I flourish.

PART THREE
Implications

Chapter 8

LETTING GO

IT WAS LATE November and my mesearch project was coming to an end. A few months before I had been terrified that I wouldn't be where I should be at the end of the project. I was still clinging to my belief that I needed to achieve my goals. However, I now understood that my undertaking was much more than a year-long project. I was on a journey, an expedition that was not signposted with objectives, goals, and timelines, but rather it was a path that was unfolding underneath me one step at a time. This path could not be bulldozed. I had to be gentle with it. The path could not be illuminated by a tour guide; it was mine to discover. In accepting this, I was learning the power of letting go. In research report terms, "letting go" was a key implication of all that I had learned. At an L3 meeting that November, I became acutely aware of the significance of this implication.

During the meeting, one of the members said he had something to show us. "I call it the 'give a shit curve,'" he said, and smiled. On a blank piece of paper, he drew a horizontal line across the bottom of the page and labelled it "age." He then drew a perpendicular line up the left side and labelled it "amount of shit given." Then he drew a line from the bottom left corner to the middle of the top of the page. During the first few decades of his life, he said, he gave a lot of shit: his business was growing exponentially, he had young kids, and he was hell-bent on success. He hovered his marker along the top of the page and then drew it down towards the bottom right corner, stopping halfway. He looked up at us with a grin and said, "This is about where I'm at now."

The group broke into laughter. For one of these high-powered achievers to proudly declare that he was giving "less of a shit" was delicious, a flagrant violation of what we were supposed to care about. As CEOs, we were all in the driver's seat and here was one of our own admitting to the enjoyment that came from taking his hands off the wheel. We resumed our meeting, but I knew what he said was meaningful. It reminded me of something I had recently read in Jon Kabat-Zinn's book, *Wherever You Go, There You Are*. "Letting go... [is] an invitation to cease clinging to anything—whether it be an idea, a thing, an event, a particular time, or view or desire. It is a conscious decision to release with full acceptance into the stream of present moments as they are unfolding. To let go means to give up coercing, resisting, or struggling, in exchange for something more powerful...."[24]

I saw the parallel between "giving less of a shit" and the concept of letting go. It wasn't that you didn't care—it meant letting go of expectations and outcomes, loosening the attachment to a goal, and finding the happiness on the way. Rather than try to wrangle life into the shape you want it to take, you had the option of expressing acceptance and curiosity instead. In effect, giving less of a shit. Kabat-Zinn's words were enticing. Give up the struggling and coercing in exchange for something more powerful.

The idea of letting go is appealing to achievers. In my survey, about two thirds say they have a hard time letting go of concerns and relaxing into life, and about half say they wish they could just let go. What holds us back? The need for control. Eighty-four percent of the surveyed achievers say that feeling like they have everything under control is very important to them. And this insight around control is a major implication of my research project. Once achievers stop believing we are in control, we can let go of needing to be in control. Letting go is not about giving up, but about giving in, surrendering to the understanding that we can't control the outcome. The "give a shit curve" brought this insight home, but it was my exploration of Buddhism that laid the initial foundation.

As I learned more about mind and meditation, I became interested in Buddhism. In my understanding, Buddhism is not a religion, but rather a field of study, a study of the mind. Mark Epstein, a psychotherapist, describes Buddhism in his book, *Going to Pieces Without Falling Apart*, as "the most psychological of the world's religions, and the most spiritual of the world's psychologies."[25] Stephen Batchelor, who wrote *Buddhism Without Beliefs*, sees Buddhism as a philosophy rather than a religion because it does not depend on beliefs. In fact, Buddhism is about a lack of beliefs because the fewer beliefs we have, the more open, peaceful, and joyful our minds become.

Based on my understanding, the Buddha was a prince who was kept cloistered in the palace courtyard. One day he decided to see what was going on beyond the palace gate and left his life of privilege. He was stunned by what he found—people suffering from old age, disease, and poverty. He realized he too would get old and suffer and this made him fearful. So, he spent years trying to control these fears. He sought out others to teach him and he engaged in a variety of exercises to strengthen his self-discipline. But escaping these fearful thoughts was an impossibility so he gave up and sat under a tree for a month. It was only when he was on his own, not listening to others, not trying to learn, not searching, not asking, eventually not even thinking, that he got to the point where he was just being, and that is when he had his big realization.

The Buddha realized that everyone suffers and that the cause of this suffering is our minds and our attachment to thoughts. We suffer because we want things to be different than what is happening. We want to control what happens as opposed to accepting what happens. We want to control how we feel. We are convinced that there is something better around the corner, that the next achievement will make things right or better, and we chase it. The Buddha, on the other hand, saw that life is always perfect right here, right now. But we develop the belief that the world is not perfect, that we are not perfect. We listen to our inner critics telling us we aren't good enough as we are and spend the rest of our lives trying to fix and control, striving ourselves crazy in the process.

Control is an illusion. Life is in constant motion. We can't control people or what they think. We can't control the market, our employees, our clients, our families. Sometimes we can't even control ourselves. A night of binge-watching or a bad hangover has made this more than apparent for me. And indeed, science has proven that everything in the known universe is made up of atoms, millions and billions of atoms, which are in constant motion. Nothing is ever stable. Our bodies die a little more each day. The weather changes every minute. Trying to control something is like trying to hold back the wind and leads only to struggle and suffering.

The mind is the cause of suffering because it is where thoughts are generated. We spend so much of our time in a state of craving for something to be better or different. If we aren't craving, we are in a state of aversion—we want something to stop, we want to get away from something. When we are attached to craving or aversion, we cannot feel the joy and peace that is always available to us.

To find that peace, we need to let go of the thought that is causing the craving or aversion. And, to help let it go, we need to recognize how fleeting the thoughts are that cross our minds. As I learned in meditation, thinking is like a never-ending train—our thoughts stream across our mind in constant motion. Whenever we grab hold of these thoughts, we can get bound up in a state of worry or fear because we have attached ourselves to them. We are frozen as the world continues to constantly move along. Only by recognizing that we are attaching or clutching can we release and move back into the world of spaciousness and growth.

This is what Byron Katie knows so well. However, she also stresses we can't just let go of painful thoughts automatically; we must question them so that we can let them go. By ignoring, burying, or wishing them away, they fester. If we want to stop clutching, we need to spend time with these painful thoughts, and ask, are they true? Katie's system, The Work, helps us to see how caught up we are in our thoughts and then to send them on their way.

The "give a shit curve" is a suffering curve. As achievers, we get attached to what we think we want and what we think we should do. We cling to these thoughts and strive and coerce and struggle to bring a goal to fruition only to realize we need to do it all over again. And again. We crave our accomplishments, but craving can only bring pain because craving never ends, it can never be satisfied. Buddhism says the same thing about pleasure, that pleasure is actually pain because we will always want more and we will never feel fulfilled. The craving and striving and struggling and coercing bolster the illusion that we are in control of the process—and that is what gives us achiever fever. When we let go, the fever goes away.

This isn't to say we sit around and do nothing. We can set a goal, or better, an intention, create a plan to bring it to life, and accept that our achiever-type qualities such as passion and persistence will kick in. Then, we can let go and be present as it all unfolds, experiencing the joy as it arises and being grateful for the tough times and the lessons and gifts they provide. We course correct from time to time but remember that we cannot control the process. My friend Mark described it like this: "When I try to control everything, the world seems bleak and full of problems, but when I let go, the world feels benevolent."

Byron Katie takes the idea a step further. When I asked why high achievers get in their own way she replied, "High achieving people have a particularly strong attachment to control. They are convinced that their way is best, and often they are right. But like all attachments, this one causes suffering and conflict, and it narrows the mind. I often ask people, 'Would you rather be right or free?'" I struggled with her words at first. I liked being "right" but, after consideration, I knew I was more effective, creative, open, and curious if I wasn't attached to "my way."

✦

AT THE END of the year, Chris and I had Ean and his wife, Shauna, over for dinner. This was my opportunity to thank him for all that he taught me, and I was full of nervous energy as I waited for them to arrive. I was going to start our evening with a bottle of wine from his favourite winery, Silver Oak, that I had purchased on a trip to Napa with my best friend a few months prior. When I bought it, I had visions of a tearful, heartfelt toast. Beware expectation. Ean arrived with a terrible cold and my energy deflated, realizing the evening would not be going according to my plan. We ate dinner quickly and Ean managed a glass. I was getting upset because I felt the need to mark the year, to symbolically end it somehow, but a toast to a sick man didn't match up with my vision. Maybe the letter would.

This was the letter I had written a year ago and stuck in my underwear drawer. I had carefully ignored it for the past year but now it was time to read it. I went to my bedroom, found the letter, and, back at the dinner table, opened it with shaking hands. I read it out loud. "Dear Claire, I am writing this to sincerely congratulate you for all that you have achieved this year. You have transformed the way you think about yourself. I know it seemed like a bit of a pipe dream back then, but you have undergone a tremendous change and instilled habits that will enable you to lead a happy, energy-filled, loving life."

I was crying before I got to the end of the first sentence. There it was, "achieved," and the word made my heart swell. I had indeed accomplished something enormous, and it was the achiever in me that had led the charge through the year—the achiever that started the project, the achiever that stuck to my three weekly sessions with Ean, the achiever that kept up the

meditation, reading, and journaling. But there was no fever evident as I read the letter. Instead, the achiever was just a participant in my personal focus group of the thinker, the wanderer,
the comedian, the coach, the creator, even that gnarled tree
stump, the Judge. They had all worked together to give me an
incredible experience.

I continued to read through the letter, stopping to sob in places,
overcome with gratitude for what had happened over the past
year: for Ean and Chris, my team at Lux, my family, and all the
people in my life that had been part of the experience. And then
I got to the last line, the line that had been so difficult to write
twelve months ago—"I love you." I read it and I knew it was true.
No achievement could ever give me what I felt in that moment. I
had found my sun and it was shining so strongly I could burst.

✦

AT LEAST TWO years before my project with Ean began, my
friend Crystal first told me about the silent retreat. As we were
driving to a climbing crag, we talked about various trips we'd
recently been on and she mentioned that she had done a ten-
day retreat—with no speaking, reading, or talking. I vividly
recall whipping my head around to gape at her. "What? Why
on earth would anyone ever want to do that? You can't read?
You can't speak? I could never do that in a million years!" Back
then, I couldn't fathom why anyone would ever want to spend
ten days in their own head.

A few years later, during the middle of my project with Ean,
I read Dan Harris's wonderful book, *10% Happier,* in which he
wrote about his experience on a silent retreat. Then I discovered that my sister's boyfriend's brother had done one a few

times. Another friend mentioned one over lunch, and then several weeks after that, someone who had seen me speak on behavioural economics wrote me an email encouraging me to sign up for one. I was feeling physically pulled towards going on such a retreat. One day at work, several months after my sessions with Ean had ended, I finally signed up. Though it meant being completely off the grid for ten days, I knew my work team would be OK without me. There was no self-doubt, no judgement, no fear—the decision felt like it was making itself. Little did I know that this retreat would deeply reinforce all that I had learned during the mesearch project.

The retreat was a Vipassana retreat. Vipassana is a form of meditation that has been around for centuries and the retreats are offered all over the world. They are run entirely on volunteer hours and donations. At the end of the ten days, you decide what, if anything, you'd like to donate. The local Vipassana website was lo-fi, but it had all the information I needed. I was shocked to see that the first availability was six months away. Obviously, these retreats were more popular than I expected, even though the site made it very clear that the retreat was not a vacation or spa.

As the six months rolled by, I didn't think about the retreat. Before my work with Ean, I would have been stressed and worried about trying something so new. As the day came closer, I began to tell friends and family about it. There was some head shaking, no doubt some considerable eye rolling, and I think my dad was concerned I was going to join a cult. Nothing anyone said gave me a moment of pause.

Packing for the retreat was easy: comfy clothes, a sleeping bag, a set of sheets, a pillow, flip flops, runners, ear plugs (I'd be sharing a room), toiletries, and bug spray. The bug spray was key because one of the retreat's rules was no killing—not even mosquitos. Some other rules were no drugs, alcohol, meat, or caffeine. No phones or technology of any sort. All those things were easy for me. The no communication with other students rule—no talking or even eye contact—would be a challenge. But the rule that scared me the most was no reading or writing. There hasn't been a day since I was about seven years old when I hadn't read something. I struggled with deciding whether to smuggle my journal in. What if I had some deep insight and I wasn't able to write it down?

I felt a quiet, powerful confidence as I drove the two and a half hours out to the retreat. I parked out front of registration, locked my journal in the glove compartment, and walked into the hustle and bustle of students. There were sixty of us: thirty men and thirty women. I was given a package of information and asked to sign a promise that I was entering a ten-day commitment and saw no reason why I could not complete it. I signed it without thought and headed off to my room.

My first surprise was that I had four roommates; I had only anticipated one or two. The room consisted of five beds with foam mattresses, each with a small bedside table and lamp. Bedsheets had been hung between the beds to give each of us privacy. An hour later we were eating dinner in the dining hall, a simple lentil soup, cornbread, and salad. Before the silence officially began, there was a lot of nervous chatter with people asking each other questions such as: Where are you from? Have you done this before? What drew you here? About two-thirds of the students were first-timers.

At eight that evening, silence began. One by one our names were called and we took our meditation cushions to an assigned spot in the meditation hall. We would be spending the next ten days in this room. After a short meditation, we headed back to our rooms in silence for lights out. My roommates and I, all between the ages of thirty-five and fifty, seemed well-meaning and respectful, and we manoeuvred around the shared bathroom and each other silently.

Three things got me out of bed at four the next morning. One, a sense of competition. The sound of my roommates rustling around motivated me to get up. Two, I was used to getting up early for swimming. Three, sheer curiosity. I dressed, grabbed my blanket, and shuffled up to the hall for the first morning meditation. I had never meditated this early before, nor for this long. The first session would last from 4:30 to 6.30 am. The novelty of this initial experience was what kept me awake throughout the first session. Finally, the gong went, and we all headed to the dining hall.

It was strange avoiding eye contact as I reached over someone's hand to grab tahini for my toast or milk for my tea, but I took the rule seriously because I wanted to extract absolutely everything I could out of the experience. That said, I did check out logos on others people's clothes, and I was soon making up stories about my fellow meditators. After breakfast, we had a short break before the next meditation period. This next session was a little shorter, an hour, and then another short break and back again for a two-hour session. As the time dragged by that first morning, I dimly started waking up to what I had signed up for—a lot of meditation.

Eventually, the gong sounded again and we all filed into lunch. We had a little free time before the next meditation session and, over the ten days, I used this time to either have a shower or walk on the small walking paths. I had to be careful because there were ants on the path and I wasn't allowed to kill any of them. That first day, watching the ants, I was excited by my ability to be present and I remember feeling a sense of pride. I also remember, within a couple of seconds of feeling proud, almost stepping on a garter snake. Shocked, I broke silence and shrieked as it slithered away into the bushes.

The gong rang again after lunch for ninety minutes of optional meditation in the hall. I spent that particular session (and many of the sessions to come) in a state of incredulity. How could I possibly do this for ten days? My muscles were starting to stiffen up from holding the same position. Most first-timers audibly sighed when the session was done, and we fell over our cushions trying to stretch out our aching backs, hips, legs, and necks. During the first few days, I spent a lot of time doing pigeon pose in the hallway, desperately trying to relieve the pain in my right hip.

There was another short break and then back into the hall for the mid-afternoon session. It was during this session when I started doing the math. Ten days of ten hours of meditation a day. I hadn't even done a tenth of it yet. My head started to spin and all I can remember from that session was feeling stunned.

At five o'clock, the gong went again and I dragged my broken body to the kitchen. Everything hurt. No stretch would make the pain go away. Teatime was fruit only; there was no other food served after lunch. Apples, bananas, oranges, pears. Ginger tea was also served, which was great for the nausea that came up on day two. Back to the hall at six for more meditation, a quick break, and then, finally, time for an hour or so of teaching.

Vipassana retreats around the world follow the same format. Their most recent global head teacher, V.S. Goenka, died in 2013, and we watched him on videotape. I quickly forgave the dated technology as I warmed to what he was saying. He had a wonderful, humorous, kind way of explaining life. It reaffirmed much of what I had been learning about in Buddhism. Goenka told us that our job at the retreat was to be aware. Aware of how our bodies felt, aware of our food, aware of how we ate, aware of our beds, our walks, what we saw, what we noticed. Also, to be aware of our thoughts. And our job was to remain equanimeous as we did. Here was a word I had heard several times before but never really understood until he explained it. Being equanimeous is simply accepting what is happening without any judgement, aversion (I'm bored. When will this end?), or clinging (This food is delicious. I hope lunchtime never ends.). Essentially, our task was to become aware of what was happening in a balanced and equanimeous way, in a state of flow, feeling calm and peaceful, and to accept whatever came up for us.

The novelty wore off on day two and the retreat became sheer, miserable drudgery. I'd finish a meditation session and think, I absolutely can't do that again. Ten minutes later, I'd be back, dreading the next two hours. I did this throughout the retreat and I was immensely grateful for my sense of discipline. There were some good sessions and some bad ones. Good in that they seemed to simply flow and I would feel light and happy and peaceful. Bad in that they were unbearably boring. The bad sessions tended to be full of anger, frustration, and irritation, but at least they ended. Good or bad, I was grateful for every session I sat through. Day four was particularly memorable.

By this point, we were expected to sit completely still for an hour at a time, no moving or fidgeting. I arranged myself on my mat, closed my eyes, and started breathing. Almost immediately I could feel pins and needles in my foot. Over the next fifteen minutes or so, the tingles crept up my leg until the whole limb was uncomfortable. I told myself to ignore it. But, the more

I tried to ignore it, the more I thought about it. "Don't think about the leg" was a constant reminder that my leg was asleep. I was dying to move my leg. Of course, the harder I willed the session to be over, the worse my leg got. I was attached to the thought of how my leg felt. The achiever in me refused to move; I was going to follow the rules and excel at this, even if it killed me. Fifteen minutes later, that's exactly what my thoughts were telling me—that my leg was going to kill me, that the blood had stopped, I was causing myself gangrene that would go into sepsis. My mind spiralled out of control, conceiving every horrible outcome. My entire body felt like it was emanating a burning, red heat. I was convinced I would not be able to walk out of the room when the session was over.

Then, the bell rang. I gingerly unfolded my leg and the pain vanished instantly. And the lesson was apparent—nothing had happened. The pins and needles came and went, but I had let my thoughts consume me. This time, I couldn't get out of my own way. In that meditation session, I saw how powerful my mind was.

As I continued through the days, I became aware of a profound feeling of gratitude. Gratitude to myself for participating each day, for taking it seriously, for not breaking any of the rules, gratitude for my parents' love and for instilling a work ethic in me, gratitude for my team not questioning my wanting to do this, gratitude for them being so capable that they didn't need me for ten days, gratitude to Chris for supporting me, gratitude for the friendship and love of my sisters. When my comforts were taken away and there was nothing at all to distract me, the result was an outpouring of love and gratitude for all the people in my life. Finding love and appreciation for myself was the impetus for that outpouring.

On day six, during my post-lunch walk, I happened to glance at a rock beside the trail and saw that someone had built a little smiley face on it with pebbles. They had taken the time to send passersby a message that we were all in this together. A surge of connection ran through me, as if someone had given me an enormous hug. As tears filled my eyes, I thought, this is what it's all about. I was reminded of the man who had sent me the flower cookies back in Seattle. He had sent me a message that he noticed and cared about me, but I had been too caught up in negative thoughts to appreciate it. How many other beautiful moments and gifts in my life had I been blind to? All along, all I had to do was open my eyes.

The best part about that smiley face is that I went to look for it the next day, but it was gone, swept away. I smiled, of course it was. Everything is constantly changing, but there I was, even at this meditation retreat, clinging to a desire to see those pebbles again rather than simply accepting the experience for what it was, a moment of beauty.

On the last day, we were finally allowed to talk. At the end of the morning meditation, the two teachers gave us a smile and left the front of the room—the silence was over. All of us continued in our positions, not knowing what came next. We had been given no instructions and I felt like a child, waiting to be told what to do. As we walked out into the hallway, I said, my voice crackling in my throat because it was so dry, "I think we can talk now." I raised my head and, for the first time in ten days, made eye contact. It was with a tall blonde woman. We looked at each other and, in a split second, something indescribably deep was exchanged. *I see you. I see you.* In that moment, I understood that calling myself an achiever had given me an identity as an individual, which had kept me at a distance from others. Now all

I could feel was love. All of us were now looking at each other, crying, laughing, utterly connected. I involuntarily brought my palm to my heart; the feeling of community was so powerful. I was deeply connected to these people. But only because I was so deeply connected to myself.

And as I drove home that day in silence (I couldn't bear to turn the radio on), I continued to feel a profound gratitude and love for everyone in my life. I was floating in a state of quiet peace and curiosity and knew I was connected to my centre, my inner self. My journal remained locked in my glove compartment. I felt no need to write anything down, there was no to-do list. All I ever needed to navigate through any decision, any situation, was all inside me.

As I neared the house, I began thinking about Chris. Would he be home? I left my bags in the car and opened the front door. "Hello?" I called out. And then he was there on the stairs and I walked up to him and convulsed into tears. The love I felt was overwhelming.

This intense feeling of love and gratitude stayed with me the rest of the day. All the flowers and vegetables that we had planted before I went on the retreat were now sprouting and, as Chris showed me the garden, everything seemed like the most amazing, beautiful thing. I kept saying, "I can't believe how gorgeous everything is!" He played me the new Arcade Fire song, which also made my cry. I remember saying, "I love that these people would spend so much time creating something so beautiful for all of us to listen to!" I had told Ean I wanted to be the sun in my own life, how I wanted to shine on the people around me, bringing warmth and love to everyone. I had seen my sun at the retreat, but thanks to what I had learned, I knew not to cling to it.

When I went to work the next morning, my team pranked me by not speaking a word or looking me in the eyes. *Of course.* Over the next few days, slowly but surely, clouds started to drift in. Within a week, the retreat was a memory. Soon, I couldn't meditate for even an hour at a time. Within a few weeks, I was down to twenty minutes a day, sometimes skipping it entirely. But I didn't get upset. This retreat was forever a part of me, accessible whenever I wanted to get quiet and still enough to reconnect and tap into what I'd learned. Love, gratitude, and letting go—the cure for achiever fever was inside me.

Chapter 9

PRACTICE

ONE RAINY NIGHT, a few months after my work with Ean had finished, I pulled into my carport and saw three huge bags of garbage in the alley behind our house. Everyone in our quadraplex always puts their garbage in bins, otherwise the raccoons destroy it. These rogue bags appeared to have been dumped. I ignored the warning feeling in my stomach and headed inside for the evening.

The next morning it was still raining and I had to run to my car to avoid getting soaked. As I pulled out of the carport, I knew before I even looked that the raccoons had paid an overnight visit, and the contents of those bags of garbage were now scattered all over the back alley. "Fuck!" I yelled in my car. Who the hell was going to clean that up? I should have dealt with them yesterday!

I drove to my workout and came back hoping some kind citizen would have cleaned up the mess, but the garbage was now sloshing around in puddles. I parked my car and went over to check it out, hands on my hips. I looked around menacingly, wondering which of my jerk neighbours had dared to foist their overflow trash on us. This isn't fair! This is not my fault! My anger slowly turned to incredulity as it dawned on me that this was now my mess to clean up. I had to deal with it because no one else would, and it was just going to get worse as the rain came down.

Again, I looked around, angry that this task was falling on me. I didn't cause any of this! With my bare hands, I scooped up wet bread, cookie wrappers, broken frying pans, used light bulbs, meat scraps, and soggy plastic. One hour later, soaking wet, I had bagged and redistributed all the garbage, managing to get most of it in the bins and the rest in my car so I could drop it off later at a dumpster. I was covered in filth and slime and absolutely furious. I got into the shower, and, as I warmed up under the hot water, I replayed the story from the moment I saw the garbage the night before, to my intuition that we were going to get a visit from the raccoons, to the ignoring of that intuition, and the resulting mess the next morning. I saw how I had used my bare hands as an expression of martyrdom.

As the hot water poured down on me, the anger faded and I started smiling, then laughing. Then, out of nowhere, I felt gratitude. Gratitude for dealing with something that no one else wanted to deal with—I was the good community citizen. Then, I felt gratitude for the people that left the bags so that I could have this experience. As I reached for the towel, I realized that the entire experience was an exercise in self-awareness. I had been watching my thoughts, staying present, and observing my reactions. I saw that, yes, I had ignored my intuition, but also that I was able to let that go and forgive myself so that I was able to find the gift and the gratitude in the experience. I could see these things as irritating or I could see them as practice.

✦

As the months rolled by after the mesearch project ended, my curiosity guided me to new authors, teachers, and retreats, and my desire to keep exploring remained strong. I was energized and confident in all aspects of my life. My business was rapidly expanding and I felt a deep sense of fulfillment. Achiever fever had released its grip, but I was also aware how easy it was to get sick again. Staying healthy required practice.

Practice. I love this word, but only recently. Practice, for me, used to be a chore: gotta get to swim practice, gotta practice my presentation. Practice was a means to an end. If I practiced, maybe I'd make swim finals, maybe I'd ace the presentation. And almost always, I would approach practice the same way— ugh, do I have to? Not practicing led to guilt and thoughts about being a lazy, weak person, so it was no surprise that I did not associate practice with enjoyment. Practice meant try harder.

Then, a few years ago, when I started doing yoga on a regular basis, I noticed that teachers would talk about their yoga practice in a different way than I was used to. They would say things like just showing up to your mat was a form of practice. To them, practice was less about working towards something and more about experiencing and accepting whatever happened during that practice and incorporating it into one's life without expectations. It was practice for the sake of practice.

This concept of practice now suits me perfectly. Practice offers a means to put in effort to support what has become important to me: self-awareness, being present, resisting the

Judge, getting from rather than getting through, feeling centred, feeling energized, being curious, being kind and generous, loving and appreciating myself, connection with and love for others, inquiring into and letting go of thoughts that are not serving me, and, most of all, enjoying my life and bringing joy to others.

So, after all this internal growth, do I live my life practicing these things every day? I try but don't always succeed. I glare at the person who has accidentally pushed their shopping cart into my leg. I sigh audibly when a retail clerk cannot accept my return. I gossip. I slam the horn on the construction vehicle blocking my car in the alley. I squirm my way through someone else's presentation convinced I could do a better job. I roll my eyes behind peoples' backs. I still get caught by the voice in my head that tells me I'm not trying hard enough or I'm an idiot and have no idea what I'm doing.

But the difference now, compared to four years ago, is that I am more likely to notice the feelings that trigger these behaviours and let them go without judgement. The worries don't hang around as long. I am quicker to recognize when I am attaching to a thought. I am more likely to catch myself when I'm not listening or unfocused. I am aware of the Judge, and when I veer into negative self-talk, I can often catch it. These changes aren't achievements. They are simply part of my ongoing practice. I want to experience life as it happens. It doesn't mean there's always brightness and light, but no matter how cloudy my day feels, I am aware that my sun is always shining. And I remind myself, again and again, that this is what I want. This is the practice.

Achiever fever feeds off an "other," someone to compare oneself against, someone to prove oneself to, someone to impress.

But I have learned that no one was keeping score or walking around with a clipboard checking off my accomplishments. Once the idea of this "other" drops away, the sickness is healed. But dropping the idea of the "other" is not easy. The need to prove myself is deeply ingrained, and my tendency to compare myself with others often flares up. However, today I'm grateful for these times because they trigger two key components of my practice: self-compassion and self-forgiveness.

Achievers have a tough time forgiving themselves. According to my survey, three quarters say it is much easier for them to forgive others than it is to forgive themselves. But if we can't forgive ourselves, we can't let go, and we remain trapped. When I find myself avoiding painful emotions and giving into distractions, using the "being too busy to meditate" excuse, or checking out of a conversation, rather than beat myself up for skipping out, or not prioritizing, or forgetting, I can see it as an opportunity to experience compassion and find forgiveness so I can start over again the next day. This part of my practice is particularly enriching because it is teaching me to find deeper compassion for others as well.

There is no denying that the concept of practice appeals to the achiever in me. Practice counts on me showing up and making decisions in accordance with what's important to me. The joy and growth from practice comes in the ability to let go of any goals and experience the practice for what it is—good, bad, boring, fun. There is nothing right or wrong in any of it. Like the yoga teachers, I now see my practice as an opportunity to appreciate having no goals and accepting whatever is happening in the moment. There is no need to apply any pressure. In fact, when pressure is applied, the practice will go awry.

The great thing about this kind of practice is that it doesn't cost anything. You can do this practice anytime, anywhere. No teacher is needed. If we can get quiet enough, if we can practice the qualities that are important, all the insights and curiosity and joy and peace and love bubble up inside of us. Certainly, there are ways to hone the practice by working with teachers and by attending retreats, for example, but the real practice is day-to-day living. Each day brings another opportunity to practice. Maybe the practice is dealing with other people's garbage. Maybe the practice is staying present as a co-worker complains. Whatever the opportunity is that arises and asks you to plug into presence, it's all practice.

◆

MARKET RESEARCH REPORTS will usually contain a recommendations section and this is my version of that section. I'm neither good nor bad at any of the practices below; they are simply what serve me at this stage of my life. But you may find an insight in one of them that inspires whatever practices make sense for you.

MEDITATION

I used to think meditation was the least productive thing one could possibly do. Now I see it as one of the most important practices in my life. It brings me home to myself, which in turn lights a fire in me to reach out to others. But it's so easy *not* to meditate. There is always a wealth of distractions calling for my attention. As a result, incorporating meditation into my life is as much of a practice as meditating itself. My intention is to meditate every day but this doesn't always work out. As such, letting go of feeling guilty for not meditating is also part of the practice.

My preferred time to meditate is in the morning, right after waking. When my alarm goes off at five, I usually want to stay in bed and I must remind myself why I want to meditate. This act alone, this "win" over the thought, is empowering (I have gotten out of my own way!) and the practice has already begun. Sometimes, I will have a wonderful session where I will settle into a deep sense of peace that I can recall at key moments throughout the day. Sometimes, I'll have a lousy meditation session where I can't settle my thoughts or stop planning my day. I get two gifts when this happens: a reminder to slow myself down and practice trying to be present the rest of the day, and an opportunity to find compassion for myself and remember that I can start again tomorrow. Either way, I can't lose.

Outside my home practice, I try to meditate with a group once a week. These group sessions always reinvigorate my commitment to meditate. Once or twice a year, I will attend a meditation retreat. Retreats are an excellent way of renewing my commitment to values like open-mindedness, awareness, connection, and compassion. There will be periods, sometimes when I travel, where my meditation practice stalls. This has happened often enough that I have learned to accept that this is what is happening right now rather than getting distressed. Usually I am pulled back to mediation when I catch myself trying to be in control, feeling rushed, not listening to others, or not being present. That's my cue to go back to the practice.

PHYSICAL EXERCISE

I've spent years calling swim practice "practice" but I didn't understand it the way I do now. Now I see swimming as the perfect way to practice all that I learned during the mesearch project. However, during the project year, I recognized that my competitive approach to swim practice was not helping me so I stopped going. Instead, I did yoga so I could learn to focus on my breathing and I also took up Kung Fu. I knew I would return to swimming when I was ready and the time came about a year after I finished working with Ean.

What I love about swimming is that it is all about breathing. When we do long sets, I'll use the opportunity to focus on my breath. My body will relax, my mind will let go, and I'll just enjoy the feeling of pulling through the water. Swimming is also a great way to practice being present. I often catch myself thinking about what time it might be, or what the next set might look like, or how many more laps I have to do in the current set. Frequently, I catch myself thinking about work. These are perfect opportunities to remind myself to come back to the present moment and focus on my breathing and technique. In this way, aside from getting a great physical workout, swim practice is no different than what I am doing when I am sitting at home meditating.

Like any kind of sports practice, there is a lot of drudgery in swimming. Sets can be repetitive and there are only four strokes to incorporate. But swim practice is only boring if I decide it's boring. When I catch myself trying to push harder by using poor technique, or comparing myself with others, I'll gently tell myself to calm down. Smiling underwater helps—it reminds me to stop taking it too seriously.

I swim with a great group of people. We've all chosen to start our day in a cold swimming pool and that leads to a special type of camaraderie. We joke with each other, but more importantly, we motivate each other. Every swim practice is an opportunity to connect with these people and this spirit of community is a joyful way to start the day. I leave the pool feeling grateful for my coach and teammates.

TRUST IN THE FLOW

Athletes will often describe themselves as being in a state of flow. A place where goals seem to score themselves, where big walls are climbed with no fear, and where runners find themselves in a zone with endless energy. I'll experience this state of flow when I am so deeply immersed in something I enjoy that I've lost all sense of time. And this is what flow is—doing without thinking. The mind shuts off and we rely on skills and experience to lead us. There is no resistance, and, in that, there is joy.

This practice of flow is about trusting that what needs to happen will indeed happen, which in turn frees us to open our eyes to what is happening right in front of us. It is not an easy practice. We are so used to wanting to feel in control of our days that it can be very difficult to take our hands off the wheel and let the day simply unfold. To me, flow is about letting go of trying to control what will happen and experiencing life as it happens instead.

In the work world, going with the flow of the conversation keeps me present. I will test myself by mentally asking what the person I am with has just said. When I can't repeat it back, I'll take a couple of deep breaths, relax my body, smile, and settle back into the conversation again. Suddenly, I am engaged, open, and curious. The conversations I can recall easily take place when I am present and engaged in what is being exchanged and nothing more.

Outside of work, I try to keep a Saturday or Sunday every month completely unplanned. I call them flow days. The practice is to leave the day open and go with whatever comes up.

Sometimes, I will simply walk to the end of my block and see which way my feet take me. Maybe I'll end up at the library and let myself feel pulled to whatever catches my attention there. If I'm travelling, I'll give myself a flow afternoon or evening and see what I stumble across. One evening in New York, my phone died and I decided to not charge it and see where my feet took me. As I walked, I remembered that a friend of mine was playing in a show that evening, and I told myself that I would stop and see the show if my walk happened to take me past the club. (I had no idea where the club was.) An hour later, I saw the place, bought a ticket at the door, and surprised the hell out of my friend.

These flow experiences feel magical and full of serendipity. I believe that when I let go and accept that I am not going to try and control the hours in front of me, desires and ideas float up from my subconscious and lead me to whatever it is I really want to do. (Maybe I wasn't aware of what I wanted or hadn't admitted it to myself.) Going with the flow is also a way of side-stepping my inner critic—the Judge doesn't have an opportunity to start griping when it doesn't know what's going on.

LANGUAGE

As I have learned to write down my stressful thoughts through inquiry, it has become apparent how often I say things like "I always" and "I never." Using language like this creates traps and becomes a self-fulfilling prophecy. The words we speak give rise to the subsequent thoughts we think.

Using different language opens up possibility. For example, rather than use the words "I hope," I replace them with "I'm curious." "I hope we make our numbers this year" becomes "I'm curious about what will happen with our numbers this year." The first statement sets out an expectation and an end goal: making our numbers. Not making our numbers means disappointment, a dashed hope. The second statement allows me to be interested in anything that happens around our numbers and thus potentially be more creative if changes need to be made. Being curious about what will happen, as opposed to expecting something to happen, takes out the worry. Living in a state of curiosity makes it much harder for the worries to worm themselves in, which frees me up to be present.

What I do now is set intentions rather than state goals. I watch my language for words like "expectation," "worry," "concern," and "what if." I watch my language for judgments and insults. I may not be able to stop my thoughts from producing these words, but not saying them out loud forces me to find another thought that feels better to express. The more I watch my language, the more aware of my thoughts I am, and the more mindfully I react.

The practice of being more thoughtful around language also changes the cadence of my speech. I take longer pauses than I used to because I am more aware of what I am going to say next, and I can decide whether or not I want to say it. Sometimes I wonder if people think I have difficulty with my memory, but I'd rather them think that than hurt their feelings with an automatic or over-emotional response. Watching my language has made me more considered and more measured, and I enjoy taking a few seconds to wait for the right word to come into my consciousness. Slowing down means I get to see my life as it happens as opposed to trying to stay ahead of it.

SELF-INQUIRY

I wrote about Byron Katie's self-inquiry system called The Work in chapter four. Today, I do The Work almost every day with a group of eight people scattered up and down the West Coast.

All eight of us attended Byron Katie's School for The Work in October of 2017. Each of us was there to learn how to inquire into and dislodge those stressful thoughts that can paralyze us. One of the attendees I spoke to described the process as "surgery" on your thinking.

Offered twice a year, The School is a nine-day retreat where participants are taught to question their beliefs through self-inquiry. A big part of the School is learning how to do inquiry with partners, also called facilitators. Facilitating someone else doing inquiry is just as powerful an experience as doing your own inquiry. As Byron Katie says, there are only so many stressful thoughts. Almost always you can relate to someone else's thoughts. The Work helps expand my mind by freeing me from limiting thoughts, and it is teaching me to find compassion for myself and others. Since there is no end to stressful thoughts, inquiry is an ongoing practice. We are human—we will keep thinking things that don't make us feel good. The Work teaches us to wake up to our passive acceptance of these thoughts and prompts us to question them. Once questioned, we are closer to being able to free ourselves from that thought. This process requires time and patience. Daily self-inquiry takes me to interior depths I had no idea existed. It has also given me seven friends with whom I am able to discuss my darkest thoughts, sometimes with excruciating honesty. It is a practice that continues to change my life.

GRATITUDE

When people ask me what the most important thing is that I've learned from my self-transformation work, gratitude is often the word that arises. I am thankful for having experienced how powerful gratitude is. However, the only time I feel it, really feel it, is when I am truly present. Whenever I sense that I *should* feel gratitude for something and subsequently try to manufacture the feeling, it doesn't work. Rather, gratitude seems to happens when I least expect it. When I had my moment in the kitchen, chopping vegetables, it was gratitude that overtook me.

Once, while I was meditating, I was deeply focused on my breath, counting "one" on my in-breath and "two" on my out-breath. A few minutes in, an image of a whale with his mouth wide open came into my mind. I saw that the whale was breathing for me, not me breathing for me. I saw that the whale represented the universe and that the universe was passing breath through me. I had nothing to do with it. And suddenly a feeling of profound gratitude to be alive vibrated through me, an experience I will never forget. But though I've had that kitchen moment and that weird whale thing, these experiences are not regular happenstances. I do believe, however, that these types of experiences are available to us any time we slow down long enough to be truly present.

I try to practice gratitude in two ways. One, when I am journaling, I will usually write three things down that I am grateful for. Some people do this every day—there are even gratitude journals available for this purpose. I am not that regular, but I do know that by keeping the awareness of gratitude front and centre in my mind, it does change my perspective. I can have an awful day and still easily find three things or people I am grateful for, even if it is just being grateful for getting to bed at a decent hour or writing in the first place. The other thing I do is to try to make eye contact with people as I walk. I don't do it all the time, but I will do it several times a week. If I do make eye contact, I am quick to smile and, almost always, so are they.

And every single time, I feel a surge of gratitude for that brief connection. Maybe they do too.

This practice has helped me open up to strangers. I will often start a conversation with someone in an elevator, for example. Yes, it can feel awkward and often I have to push myself because shyness wants to take over. But almost every time, I've found that people are happy to have a quick exchange. When strangers engage, whether it be with a sentence or a smile, it brings me joy, and that's a truly worthwhile practice.

WRITING

All my life I have written in a journal. When I was a kid I'd document my swim workouts, detail what I ate for dinner, and then write about school, boys, and my sisters. Throughout university and my marriage, I wrote less often and usually just when I was going through something difficult. After my divorce, I wrote constantly, filling journal after journal with emotional pain. When Chris and I went travelling, I wrote reviews of all the books I read and kept a blog detailing our trip. When I started my company, my writing stopped. Then five years later, round about the time I realized I was becoming a liability to my business, I started again.

I kept journals the whole time I was working with Ean. As I read book after book about awareness, self-realization, and Buddhism, I wrote constantly. I used writing as a way of grappling with concepts and ideas. I wrote to explain things to myself, as writer and reader having a conversation. And this, for me, is the real practice of writing—it keeps me connected to myself. It is the practice of listening to myself, engaging with myself, understanding myself, teaching myself. By letting my pen move of its own accord or letting my fingers fly across the keys, I'm channelling what's inside me, stuff that I'm not even aware of until it ends up on the page.

Someone once told me that writers get to live twice. Once when life happens and again when it gets put on paper. I agree with this. Take my childhood swim workouts as an example. I would have suffered through an afterschool workout and experienced the monotony that sets in with every swim practice. But later in the evening, as I carefully transcribed the workout sets, I would relive those laps and feel proud that I had done them.

This book is not dissimilar. I have lived so many interesting experiences over the last few years. Journaling them at the time, I'd better understand what I learned. Now, writing about them again in this book, I get to relive them, remember what I learned from them, and then, best of all, I get to fit all those experiences together to learn even more. At the same time, I'm deepening my connection with myself. Maybe, deepening my connection with you.

GENEROSITY

When we are generous with ourselves, we can be generous with others. My continued exploration of my inner world has led to an ability to find compassion and generosity in myself. It still feels very new and raw and the Judge usually tries to shut it down. But I can sidestep the Judge by showing generosity to others and, when I do, I feel generous towards myself in return.

I remember listening to a woman on *The One You Feed* podcast talking about how generosity at first feels like a pinch, meaning that if it doesn't hurt a little bit, it's not really generosity. I like playing with this idea and testing myself by looking for the pinch. For example, sometimes, if I pass a homeless person on the street and know I have cash in my wallet, I will take

out an amount that gives me the pinch. Or, if I make a donation to charity, I'll try to go up to just a little more than feels
comfortable.

The practice of generosity is not just money-oriented. There
are all sorts of situations where I feel a pinch if someone asks
me to do something and I want to say no. Again, that pinch is
my cue. For example, I was writing on a Greyhound bus and I
only had thirty percent of my laptop battery left. A kid leaned
over and asked if he could plug his phone into my computer so
he could charge it. I immediately felt a pinch because I believed
it would drain my battery, and then I saw that he didn't have the
right plug for my laptop anyway. Now I could say no and feel OK
about it. But then I remembered I had an adaptor that would
connect his phone to my laptop. The pinch got stronger and I
saw the opportunity to practice being generous. I charged his
phone and still managed to have enough battery to write for the
rest of the trip.

I now enjoy looking for opportunities to be generous. I don't
always act on them—sometimes I simply can't get past the pinch
and sometimes I believe that I can't provide what is needed—
but not acting on this desire to be generous gives me something
to ponder, write about, and eventually bring to self-inquiry. In
this way, the practice feeds itself and I'm curious to see how this
practice evolves.

✦

THESE ARE MY practices right now. Don't get me wrong—
many, many times I don't want to engage with any of them. At
least a couple of nights a week, I want to collapse on my couch
and watch Netflix with a huge bowl of popcorn. And sometimes

I do just that and open up a bottle of wine to boot. Sometimes I'll skip meditation and just eat chips. Sometimes I will feel a worry so deeply that I can't even bring myself to do inquiry on it. Sometimes my thoughts are just all-consuming and I'll put up with the anger, indigestion, and sleepless nights that they bring.

None of these practices are easy. But each day that I forget to be present, ignore everyone in the elevator, or catch myself running through my to-do list in the middle of a conversation, is an opportunity to remember. Each day is an opportunity to begin again. In fact, each *moment* is an opportunity to begin again. These practices, and the forgiveness that comes with screwing up these practices, help me to discover how much love I do have for myself, and, subsequently, for others. And when I forget, I just remember to remember. All the good stuff—the awareness, being present, the love and connection with myself and others, the groundedness and curiosity and wonder—it's always there, always there to be remembered. No matter how much fog rolls in, my sun is always shining.

EPILOGUE

I LOVE EPILOGUES. I love them in the same way I love the "where are they now?" spreads in celebrity magazines. And, in the case of memoir/self-help books, I love to find out if any of what the writer learned actually worked and whether or not it continues to influence their life. The best way for me to demonstrate the results of my personal transformation is to give you a sense of where I am today, four years after throwing my hands up in the air and saying, *enough*! I have got to get out of my own way!

Cooling my achiever fever has led to significant growth for my company, Lux Insights. Since I began the project, we have been commissioned to conduct research for some of the most recognizable brands in the world and revenue is up over sixty percent. More recently, I set an intention to significantly increase the size of our Seattle business and have since doubled our US staff. We have a couple of awards now as well, me as a top-three finalist for my city's business person of the year in 2016, and the team winning the 2018 North American Qually Award, which recognizes excellence in qualitative research design. My favourite story about that award is that I tried to talk my team out of applying for it because I believed that we were too busy. The team ignored me and persisted—what a great learning experience.

Growth is obviously still important for us at Lux Insights. We want to keep growing the business and ourselves, but now I see Lux less as a vehicle for financial growth and more as a community hub where we can have a positive impact on each other and the people around us. I am excited and curious to find out where the company will lead us and what it will teach me and the team.

This ongoing journey of self-discovery and transformation has greatly empowered me and, as a result, I want my team to have access to the same experiences. For example, anyone on the team is free to do a ten-day meditation retreat and is not required to use up vacation time to do so. I will also subsidize anyone who wants to attend the School for The Work or a similar program. All members of my leadership team now work with a coach because I see the importance of having someone to ask them questions, see through biases, and provoke self-reflection. The work my team members are doing individually with their coaches has deepened the level of conversation and led to more transparent and caring communication in the company. The coaching and self-empowerment also trickles down to junior members of the team, which in turn motivates the leadership team. When I was taking too long to get back to a client, a new junior employee kindly took me to task. "I thought responsiveness was a key part of our culture," she said. I gave her a hug, delighted that she cared enough about our clients to call out the owner.

The inner work I've done has left me feeling lush and verdant, like a forest springing back to life after a wildfire. No longer striving, I am now thriving, and more than that, I am flourishing. The word flourishing is more meaningful and useful to me than happiness. I realized the difference when I read an article comparing the two words through a question posed to a parent: is your child happy in school or is your child flourishing?[26] In fact, this is now the purpose of our company: Lux Insights fosters flourishing.

Flourishing makes good business as well as personal sense. As Lux flourishes, so too do our clients and our vendors. We bring the feeling of flourishing home to our families, inspiring them. As the heart (and I recognize the importance of the word and do not use it lightly) of this company, it is my responsibility to live this purpose. My primary job at Lux is to foster flourishing and that looks different for each employee. For one employee, flourishing meant moving out of her childhood home and working for us remotely in Paris for two years. For another, it meant a two-month sabbatical in Africa. Four years ago, I would have been annoyed by losing an employee for two months. Now I see what she, and subsequently the company, gains through her rich experience. For Hanson, flourishing at work means he needs my job. As of January 2019, Hanson is the new president of the company with me moving into an advisory CEO role. Letting go may not come easy—I'm curious to see how it unfolds.

While my practices keep the fever away, it will occasionally flare up. About eighteen months ago, when my company was having an abnormally slow quarter, coupled with an unpropitious pipeline, I had one or two nights similar to the scene with which I opened this book. However, unlike I would have done a couple of years previous, I did not distract myself from my fear with additional exercise, food, or wine. Instead, I let myself feel the fear and the worry and watched my left-brain interpreter paint the bleakest picture it possibly could. Instead of trying to hide how I felt, I was open with my team. I went for a walk with my co-worker Lauren and told her that I was concerned that my writing had taken my focus away from the business. I asked her if she thought I should put the book on hold and turn my attention to doubling down on business development. She thought about it for a few minutes and then told me if I did that, not only would it show the team I didn't trust them to carry the business, giving up on the book would also be sending a discouraging message. In that moment, Lauren was the perfect teacher and I felt my energy roar back.

Today my focus has transformed from growing the company to finding ways to foster its flourishing. As I discovered in my work with Ean, once I found love and generosity for myself, I could find it more easily for others. This year, it became very apparent to me that Lux Insights should do something to contribute beyond our four walls. As a team, we discussed what this might look like and settled on female empowerment. We then turned our attention to finding an organization that made sense for us to support. It was important to me that we give financially (feeling that pinch was my cue to know how much), but more importantly, that we give our time. We decided to do this with G Day, an annual one-day event that celebrates the transition from childhood to adolescence for girls, ages ten to twelve. The purpose is to foster self-acceptance, confidence, and connection by celebrating exactly who they are.

On a sunny day in May, I watched my team engage with a hundred pre-teen girls, listening as intently to the speakers as the girls were themselves. One speaker, a woman named Anna Soole, talked about our inner monster, the one that tells us mean things about ourselves. I could see the girls nodding their heads—they knew what she was talking about. The speaker then described the voice in a potent way: our inner monster is just a little kid dressed up in a monster costume. If the girls remembered this, they would not have to follow the "monster" in their heads and could develop strong self-esteem.

Meanwhile, my own monster, the Judge, still manufactures spectacularly creative thoughts to keep me in a state of "protective" self-doubt, but I am now more likely to marvel at how sneaky and imaginative it can be than to follow its direction on autopilot. I continue to learn to listen to my inner self, what some might call intuition, and do what feels right. That process feels more like a pull than a push.

Writing this book was largely a pull, but many times I wanted to quit. At one point, while I was travelling for work in New York and conducting in-home interviews for a client, I was also trying to write the questions for the achiever fever survey. Not only was I grappling with the belief that I was over-extended, exposing myself through those survey questions about self-doubt and inner voices terrified me. The prospect of launching the survey gave me two sleepless nights and a T-shirt so wet from tossing and turning I had to wring it out in the bathroom sink. Staying awake, however, gave me plenty of time to observe my behaviour and my thoughts—I was suffering from a full-blown case of achiever fever. The irony was delicious. How could I write about a cure for achiever fever when I was still suffering from the sickness? "You're an imposter!" the Judge screamed.

But, by applying my burgeoning growth mindset, I could see a much more useful experience in those wakeful nights. I got to experience the fever as a reminder of the list of symptoms I was going to write into my survey. Needing to prove oneself? Focusing on the future? Worry and anxiety? Check, check, double check. I let the fever burn me up, and then I wrote a survey that became one of the most useful parts of this book. Once the survey was launched, the fever was replaced by curiosity and I let go.

Then there were the times that I would wake up in the middle of the night suddenly terrified that I was exposing myself in a way I could never undo. I would sit up, my breath shallow, and feel a sharp tightness in my chest. What if my family, what if Chris, thought I was just a navel-gazing, verbose, self-absorbed embarrassment? I'd sit with that fear for a few minutes, not wishing it away, and, with Chris asleep beside me, take some deep breaths and watch the Judge at work. I'd ask myself, is that enough of a reason to stop writing the book? And the answer was always no. Not only was the content of the book my medicine, the act of writing it was too. The process was teaching me resilience.

As I remember my downward spirals, my sleepless nights, my self-doubt, my worrying, my battle with the Judge, my incessant planning and scheduling, my fear and self-loathing, I see that I was building resilience and resilience was building me. Had I been ready to grasp the concept ten years ago, resilience might have taken me in a different direction. But back then I saw resilience as being tough or thick-skinned. Now I see that resilience needed to be developed in the "burning"—in the crucible of fear, anxiety, depression, and insomnia. I was blind to the need for that process then. Having had those experiences and seeing that they only made me stronger, in the most warm, compassionate sense of the word, is what allows me to find the humour and love in day-to-day life.

Soon it will be ten years since Chris and I got back from our round-the-world travels, and it will be time to take another trip.

This time I'm excited to pack myself along for the journey and take my practices on the road as well. I'll make new friends, write new stories, let go, and get lost so that I can continue to find. Given all the trips, internal and external, I have taken in the past few years, I have become one of my favourite travel companions. And who wouldn't want to travel with their best friend?

ACKNOWLEDGEMENTS

Several people were instrumental in helping bring *The Achiever Fever Cure* to life.

I could not have written this book without the encouragement and support of my team at Lux Insights: Hanson Lok, Lauren McCrae, Jeff Jefkins, Jay Levinger, Nika Kabiri, Frankie Aeng, Carmen Chang, Jacquie Carten, Mike Butler, Nicole Aleong, Alexis Morton, Dave Prestage, and Carrie Finlay. You fostered my flourishing. A special thank you to Hanson Lok for being my close friend and confidant.

The spark for this book came from a conversation I had with Ean Kramer. When I told him I had kept careful notes throughout my experience working with him, he said, "Of course! For the book you're going to write!" He knew before I did that I would write it. Ean taught me how to be stronger than I think, and, as my friend and guide, showed me a different approach to life. Thanks also to Ean's wife, Shauna Barnes Kramer, for encouraging me to write and assuring me that "free falling is a good thing."

My publishing and editorial team at Lifetree Media: Maggie Langrick, Sarah Brohman, Jesmine Cham, Zoe Grams, Heather Wood, Greg Tabor, and Michelle MacAleese. Special thanks to Sarah for her thoughtful, respectful, and surgical editing. I could not have asked for a better first experience as an author. And thanks to Maggie for appealing to the achiever in me by looking me in the eyes at our first meeting and asking, "So are you going to do this?" How could I say no?

L3, my CEO peer group, for their encouragement and for holding me accountable to seeing the book through.

Karin Nieszzeri for her support of Lux Insights and for her friendship and counsel.

My newfound Sangha that will keep me burning, under the guidance of Tania and Pedro. A special thank you to Dr. Lara Patriquin for her contributions to chapter three and for connecting me to Stephen Mitchell, Byron Katie, and Derek Bullen. Thanks also to my first readers, Jody Shakespeare and Walt Sutton. It was Walt who first encouraged me to think of my company as a community.

Is it true that my The Work group—Mark, Sarah, Dave, Rebecca, Beth, Rashmi, Melissa, and Naomi—has been a support pillar throughout this process? This is one belief I am holding onto. A special thank you to Mark Diller for his writing advice and for giving me one of my favourite lines of the whole book.

My best friends—Jessica Leask, Heather Harley, and Janet O'Brien—for twenty-plus years of friendship. When I made the decision to write the book, it was Jessica I texted first, as I brushed my teeth. Woos, this is the real journal.

My parents, Ken and Ruth Booth, for quietly encouraging the achiever without giving me the fever. That part was all me. My parents have always been my role models and this book exists because they taught me to take the initiative.

My sisters, Kate Schafer and Esther Booth, for their dark and delicious humour that continues to light my spark, and for showing me what resilience looks like.

And finally, my partner, Chris Falk, who has been there for me at every stage of the conceptualization and writing of this book and who has given me fifteen years of love and support through my funks and my fears. Vanessa is calling us.

NOTES

1. Alain de Botton, *The Art of Travel* (New York: Vintage, 2002), 20.
2. The name seemed too good not to already exist and an online search led me to this article: Emma Rees, "Self-Reflective Study: The Rise of Mesearch," *Times Higher Education*, (March 19, 2015), www.timeshighereducation.com/features/self-reflective-study-the-rise-of-mesearch/2019097.article.
3. Claire Booth, "I want Comedian Louis C.K. on my Research Team!" *QRCA Views* (Fall 2016): 14-16.
4. Since the writing of this book, my belief that comedians can be incredibly insightful has only strengthened, particularly after seeing Hannah Gadsby's live performance of *Nanette* in the spring of 2018. Her comedy special on Netflix is a must-see.
5. Dr. Laura Patriquin has written on the left-brain interpreter in her blog on her Thinking2point0 site, www.thinkingtwopoint0.com/single-post/2018/06/23/The-Left-Brain-Interpreter.
6. David Wolman, "The Split Brain: A Tale of Two Halves," *Nature* (March 14, 2012): 260-263.
7. Michael Gazzaniga, *The Ethical Brain* (New York: Harper Collins, 2005), 145-155.
8. Lara Patriquin, www.thinkingtwopoint0.com/single-post/2018/06/23/The-Left-Brain-Interpreter.
9. There is no definitive percentage on conscious versus unconscious cognitive activity. Dr. Emanuel Donchin, Professor Emeritus of Psychology

at the University of Illinois, says "An enormous portion of cognitive activity is nonconscious.... Figuratively speaking, it could be 99 percent; we probably will never know precisely." Daniel Goleman, "New View of Mind Gives Unconscious an Expanded Role," *New York Times* (February 7, 1984), www.nytimes.com/1984/02/07/science/new-view-of-mind-gives-unconscious-an-expanded-role.html.

10. Colin Camerer, "Behavioral Economics: Reunifying Psychology and Economics," *Proceedings of the National Academy of Sciences* 96, no. 19 (September 14, 1999): 10575-10577.

11. Moritz Loewenfeld, "A Short History of Behavioural Economics," *TSEconomist*, (September 20, 2017), www.tseconomist.com/2017/09/20/a-short-history-of-behavioural-economics.

12. For a deeper understanding, see Daniel Kahneman, *Thinking, Fast and Slow* (New York: Farrar, Straus and Giroux, 2011).

13. See Hara Estroff Marano, "Our Brain's Negative Bias," *Psychology Today* (June 20, 2003), www.psychologytoday.com/ca/articles/200306/our-brains-negative-bias, and Brian Scott, "Our Innate Bias to Focus on the Negative and how to Compensate for its Effects," *Psychology Matters* (September 18, 2013), www.psychologymatters.asia/article/143/our-innate-bias-to-focus-on-the-negative-and-how-to-compensate-for-its-effects.html.

14. Byron Katie and Stephen Mitchell, *Loving What Is: Four Questions That Can Change Your Life* (New York: Harmony Books, 2002), ix.

15. Byron Katie and Stephen Mitchell, *Loving What Is: Four Questions That Can Change Your Life* (New York: Harmony Books, 2002), ix.

16. Eckhart Tolle, *The Power of Now* (Novato, CA: New World Publishing, 1999), 4.

17. Brigid Schulte, "Harvard neuroscientist: Meditation not only reduces your stress, here's how it changes your brain," *The Washington Post* (May 26, 2015), www.washingtonpost.com/news/inspired-life/wp/2015/05/26/harvard-neuroscientist-meditation-not-only-reduces-stress-it-literally-changes-your-brain.

18. Sarah Knapton, "Mindfulness as good as anti-depressants for tackling depression," *The Telegraph* (April 21, 2015), www.telegraph.co.uk/news/health/news/11550766/Mindfulness-as-good-as-anti-depressants-for-tackling-depression.html.

19. Carolyn Ellis, *The Ethnographic I: A Methodological Novel about Autoethnography* (Walnut Creek: AltaMira Press, 2004), 6, and Garance Maréchal, "Autoethnography," in *Encyclopedia of Case Study Research*,

ed. Albert J. Mills, Gabrielle Durepos & Elden Wiebe (Thousand Oaks, CA: Sage Publications, 2010), Vol. 2, 43-45.

20. Jon Kabat-Zinn, *Wherever You Go, There You Are* (New York: Hyperion, 1994), 14.

21. Carol Dweck, *Mindset: The New Psychology of Success* (New York: Ballantyne Books, 2006), 6.

22. Carol Dweck, *Mindset: The New Psychology of Success* (New York: Ballantyne Books, 2006), 7.

23. Carol Dweck, *Mindset: The New Psychology of Success* (New York: Ballantyne Books, 2006), 6.

24. Jon Kabat-Zinn, *Wherever You Go, There You Are* (New York: Hyperion, 2005), 53.

25. Mark Epstein, *Going to Pieces Without Falling Apart* (New York: Broadway Books, 1998), 16.

26. Richard Layard, "*Flourish: A New Understanding of Happiness and Well-Being—and How to Achieve Them* by Martin Seligman—review," *The Guardian* (May 14, 2011), www.theguardian.com/science/2011/may/15/flourish-science-of-happiness psychology-review.

BIBLIOGRAPHY

Ariely, Dan. *Predictably Irrational: The Hidden Forces that Shape our Decisions*. New York: Harper Perennial, 2008.

Batchelor, Stephen. *Buddhism Without Beliefs: A Contemporary Guide to Awakening*. New York: Riverhead Books, 1997.

Booth, Claire. "I want Comedian Louis C.K. on my Research Team!" *QRCA Views* (Fall 2016):14-16.

Camerer, Colin. "Behavioral Economics: Reunifying Psychology and Economics." *Proceedings of the National Academy of Sciences* 96, no. 19 (September 14, 1999): 10575-10577.

Chodron, Pema. *How to Meditate: A Practical Guide to Making Friends with Your Mind*. Boulder: Sounds True, 2013.

Dass, Ram. *Be Here Now*. New Mexico: Lama Foundation, 1971.

De Botton, Alain. *The Art of Travel*. New York: Vintage, 2002.

Dweck, Carol S. *Mindset: The New Psychology of Success*. New York: Ballantyne, 2006.

Epstein, Mark, M.D. *Going to Pieces Without Falling Apart: A Buddhist Perspective on Wholeness*. New York: Broadway Books, 1999.

Gazzaniga, Michael. *The Ethical Brain*. New York: Harper Collins, 2005.

Goleman, Daniel. "New View of Mind Gives Unconscious an Expanded Role." *New York Times*, February 7, 1984.

Harris, Dan. *10% Happier: How I Tamed the Voice in My Head, Reduced Stress Without Losing My Edge, and Found Self-Help That Actually Works—A True Story*. New York: HarperCollins, 2014.

Kabat-Zinn, Jon. *Wherever You Go, There You Are: Mindfulness Meditation in Everyday Life*. New York: Hyperion, 1994.

Kahneman, Daniel. *Thinking, Fast and Slow*. New York: Farrar, Strauss and Giroux, 2011.

Katie, Byron, and Stephen Mitchell. *Loving What Is: Four Questions That Can Change Your Life*. New York: Harmony, 2002.

Knapton, Sarah. "Mindfulness 'as good as anti-depressants for tackling depression.'" *The Telegraph*, April 21, 2015.

Kristeva, Julia. *Strangers to Ourselves*. Translated by Leon S. Roudiez. New York: Columbia University Press, 1991.

Layard, Richard. "*Flourish: A New Understanding of Happiness and Well-Being—and How to Achieve Them* by Martin Seligman—review." *The Guardian*, May 14, 2011.

Loewenfeld, Moritz. "A Short History of Behavioural Economics." *TSEconomist*, September 20, 2017.

Marano, Hara Estroff. "Our Brain's Negative Bias." *Psychology Today*, June 20, 2003.

Millman, Dan. *Way of the Peaceful Warrior*. Novato, CA: New World Library, 1980.

Rees, Emma. "Self-Reflective Study: The Rise of Mesearch." *Times Higher Education*, March 19, 2015.

Schulte, Brigid. "Harvard neuroscientist: Meditation not only reduces your stress, here's how it changes your brain." *The Washington Post*, May 26, 2015.

Scott, Brian. "Our Innate Bias to Focus on the Negative and how to Compensate for its Effects." *Psychology Matters*, September 18, 2013.

Tolle, Eckhart. *The Power of Now*. Novato, CA: New World Library, 1999.

Wolman, David. "The Split Brain: A Tale of Two Halves." *Nature*, March 14, 2012.

RECOMMENDED SOURCES

Books:

Bach, Richard. *Illusions: The Adventures of a Reluctant Messiah*. New York: Dell Publishing, 1977.

Chodron, Pema. *The Wisdom of No Escape*. Boulder: Shambhala Publications, 2001

Frankl, Viktor E. *Man's Search for Meaning*. Boston: Beacon Press, 1959.

Gilbert, Elizabeth. *Big Magic: Creative Living Beyond Fear*. New York: Riverhead Books, 2015.

Goldberg, Natalie. *Writing Down the Bones*. Boulder: Shambhala Publications, 1986.

Grosso, Chris. *Indie Spiritualist*. New York: Atria, 2014.

Harris, Sam. *Waking Up: A Guide to Spirituality without Religion*. New York: Simon & Schuster, 2014.

Hesse, Hermann. *Siddhartha*. New York: Bantam, 1951.

Kerouac, Jack. *Dharma Bums*. New York: Viking Press, 1958.

Levine, Noah. *Dharma Punx*. New York: HarperOne, 2003.

Millman, Dan. *Sacred Journey of the Peaceful Warrior*. Novato, CA: New World Library, 1991.

Roach, Geshe Michael. *The Diamond Cutter: The Buddha on Strategies for Managing Your Business and Your Life*. New York: Doubleday, 2000.

Singer, Michael A. *The Surrender Experiment*. New York: Harmony, 2015.

Tolle, Eckhart. *A New Earth*. New York: Plume, 2005.

Watts, Alan W. *The Book: On the Taboo Against Knowing Who You Are.*
    New York: Vintage, 1966.
Yogananda, Paramahansa. *Autobiography of a Yogi.* New York: The
    Philosophical Library, 1946.

Documentaries:
Awake: The Life of Yogananda. Directed by Paola di Florio and
    Lisa Leeman, 2014.
Happy. Directed by Roko Belic, 2011.
I Am. Directed by Tom Shadyac, 2011.
I Am Not Your Guru. Directed by Joe Berlinger, 2016.
Kumare. Directed by Vikram Gandhi, 2011.
Samsara. Directed by Ron Fricke, 2011.

Podcasts:
Essential Conversations, with Rabbi Rami.
The Indie Spiritualist Podcast, with Chris Grosso.
On Being, with Krista Tippett.
The One You Feed, with Eric Zimmer.

My teachers' websites:
Ean Kramer: www.lngvt.com
Tania Fierro and Pedro Cortina (Innerland): www.innerland.com

INDEX

Index

M

Madanes, Cloé, 142

market research: background research, 15, 29; ethnography, 121–22; focus groups, 55–57, 63; future orientation of, 98; project structure, 8; for self-discovery, 10; types of responses sought by, 6, 80

McCrae, Lauren, 194

meditation: achievers on, 123; avoidance of, 121, 122–23; beginner's mind and expectations, 131–32; brain and health impacts, 120–21; in corporations, 121; criteria for, 124; drop-in groups while travelling, 139–40; first experiences with, 124–26, 126–28; group meditation, 128–31, 180; Kabat-Zinn on, 143; lessons from, 132; mindfulness and, 134–35; one-day retreat, 132–36; as practice, 136–38, 179–80; ten-day retreat, 164–73; thoughts and, 137; train analogy, 126–27; Vipassana meditation, 165; waterfall metaphor, 137

Mesearch project: achiever fever in, 86, 96–97; author's growth during, 86, 96, 141–42, 157, 163–64, 192 93, 196; book writing experience, 9–10, 11, 195–96; continuation of, 176; discovery of personal sun, 76–77, 95, 164; end-of-year dinner, 163; future letter to self, 48–51, 124, 163–64; methodology, 9, 122; personal transformation program with Ean, 7–8, 43–48; starting point, 15 16. *See also* growth; inner critic; Judge; letting go; meditation; practice; present, being; thoughts

Michelangelo, 95

Millman, Dan: *Way of the Peaceful Warrior*, 120

mindfulness, 134–35

mindfulness-based stressed reduction (MBSR), 143

mindset, 146–49

motivation, 29–30, 30–31, 32

mountain biking, 148

N

Nature's Path, 121

negativity bias, 85

O

The One You Feed (podcast), 70–71, 85, 123, 146, 188

others, comparison to, 177–78

P

parents, 30

Patriquin, Lara, 72, 73–74, 75, 93, 114

phones, 107–8

physical exercise, 180–82

planning, 97–98. *See also* future orientation; goal orientation

pleasure, 162

Index

CLAIRE BOOTH is an entrepreneur, author, and speaker. She is the founder and CEO of market research firm Lux Insights, with more than eighteen years' experience serving some of the world's most recognized brands. She teaches at the UBC Sauder School of Business, swims with the Northshore Masters team, and enjoys hiking and climbing all over the world. She lives with her partner, Chris, in North Vancouver, Canada.

claireboothauthor.com